REVELATION
of Jesus Christ

The Answer to WHY? Verified Scientifically as Energy, Mass and Light

Connie Jean Allen

And God saw every thing that he had made, and, behold, it was very good. And the evening [gluon strong nuclear, neon] and the morning [proton strong Gravity, hydrogen and helium] were the sixth day [radon, the six noble gases].

Genesis 1:31 KJV

Michelangelo, Last Judgment (Center Detail)

1535-1541

There are three Jewels, the physical representations of the three force particles within the nucleus of Atom Lambda. The three Jewels are Judah (proton), Israel (gluon), and Jerusalem (neutron). These three are the visible image of the forces of life: strong Gravity, gluon strong nuclear and the electroweak-weak interaction respectively.

In the center, Jesus Christ is Atom Lambda, the visible image of strong Gravity, the single force that created the universe. All other forces came to be by strong Gravity's hands, hydrogen and helium; proton and the Higgs boson. Atom Lambda made and is the first male person, Adam, his namesake. Beside him is the first female Adam, as he made Adam a male and a separate female. Adam the female is Sarah and Constance, the woman who fought the dragon.

> 2 Male and female created he them; and blessed them, and called their name Adam, in the day when they were created. Genesis 5:2 KJV

Just below, on the right hand of Christ is the strong nuclear interaction, gluon and Israel. Born of proton in period two of the periodic table of elements, gluon is self-lit. She is fueled on the noble gas neon. The coat of many colors that Isaac gave Joseph is evidence reflecting gluon's Gell-Mann octet. Gluon is Israel, Eve, the mother of all peoples, taken from Adam's rib, his deoxyRIBonucleic acid. By the strong nuclear interaction, whose coupling constant is electricity, gluon sparks movement in particle masses and people. And being Eve, mother of all, gluon is Jacob's genetic ladder. Gluon is the mother of the archetypes: the eukaryotes, the living ones: proton (Judah) and gluon (Israel). She bears the archaic ones: neutron (Jerusalem). And gluon also bears the prokaryotes, the undead quarks of electricity) conjoined with the living antiquarks of magnetism. The prokaryotes are the Gentiles, also known as Ephesus and Sardis, Cain and Abel conjoined as one mind. These do not appear in the nucleus of Atom Lambda. They do not appear in the original blueprint of life.

On the left hand of Christ, neutron sits behind the weak or electroweak interaction. He is an "either-or" force of nature; and by his two lights, Z or W+, you never quite know to whom you are speaking. Here he is shown shedding his electroweak persona for the weak force. He is Abraham, the father of all, the neutral one, whose reasoning comes by way of the gravitational field, while his sudden expressions of rage and debauchery come from the electromagnetic field. As a special unitary group, SU(2), he is the Z or W boson. As SU(3), he is Z boson, photon and W boson, a grand unification, whose mass is neutron and who's mind is named Jerusalem.

Tell Them for Us | TellThem.Us

http://iUniverse.com/author/Connie Allen

IMAGE ACQUISITION

Downloaded Images: Wikimedia Commons, licensed according to the Creative Commons Attribution-ShareAlike.

Purchased images: Licensed by Envato, Photodune, iStock Photos,

Constance illustrated by Eve Myles

Woman with Dragon illustrated by Triniti

SCRIPTURAL TEXT

The King James Version Bible (KJV) was authorized by King James I and is often referred to as the "Authorized Version," Translated by the Church of England, it was first published in 1611.

Scriptures are clarified by brackets [ ] by Connie J. Allen

Contents

REVELATION OF JESUS CHRIST
THE ANSWER TO WHY? VERIFIED SCIENTIFICALLY ENERGY, MASS AND LIGHT

iUniverse books may be ordered through booksellers or by contacting:

iUniverse
1663 Liberty Drive
Bloomington, IN 47403
www.iuniverse.com
1-800-Authors (1-800-288-4677)

ISBN: 978-1-5320-3386-5 (sc)
ISBN: 978-1-5320-3387-2 (e)

Print information available on the last page.

iUniverse rev. date: 10/27/2017

About the Author

I am Connie (Constance) Allen. In 2002, I was given to read, decode and illustrate the book of revelation for delivery at the end of this age, the age of the Gentiles. I am the one whose eyes are open, who has an ear to hear what the spirit is saying to the churches. I am the woman in labour chosen to fight the dragon, death, for life.

CONSTANCE WORKING THE PUZZLE
1977

"At that time Jesus answered and said, I thank thee, O Father, Lord of heaven and earth, because thou hast hid these things from the wise and prudent, and hast revealed them unto babes. Even so, Father: for so it seemed good in thy sight.

All things are delivered unto me of my Father: and no man knows the Son, but the Father; neither knows any man the Father, save the Son, and he to whomsoever the Son will reveal him.

Come unto me, all ye that labour and are heavy laden, and I will give you rest. Take my yoke upon you, and learn of me; for I am meek and lowly in heart: and ye shall find rest unto your souls. For my yoke is easy, and my burden is light."

Matthew 11:25-30 KJV

Understanding Life

Beginnings

Strong Gravity, The Behemoth

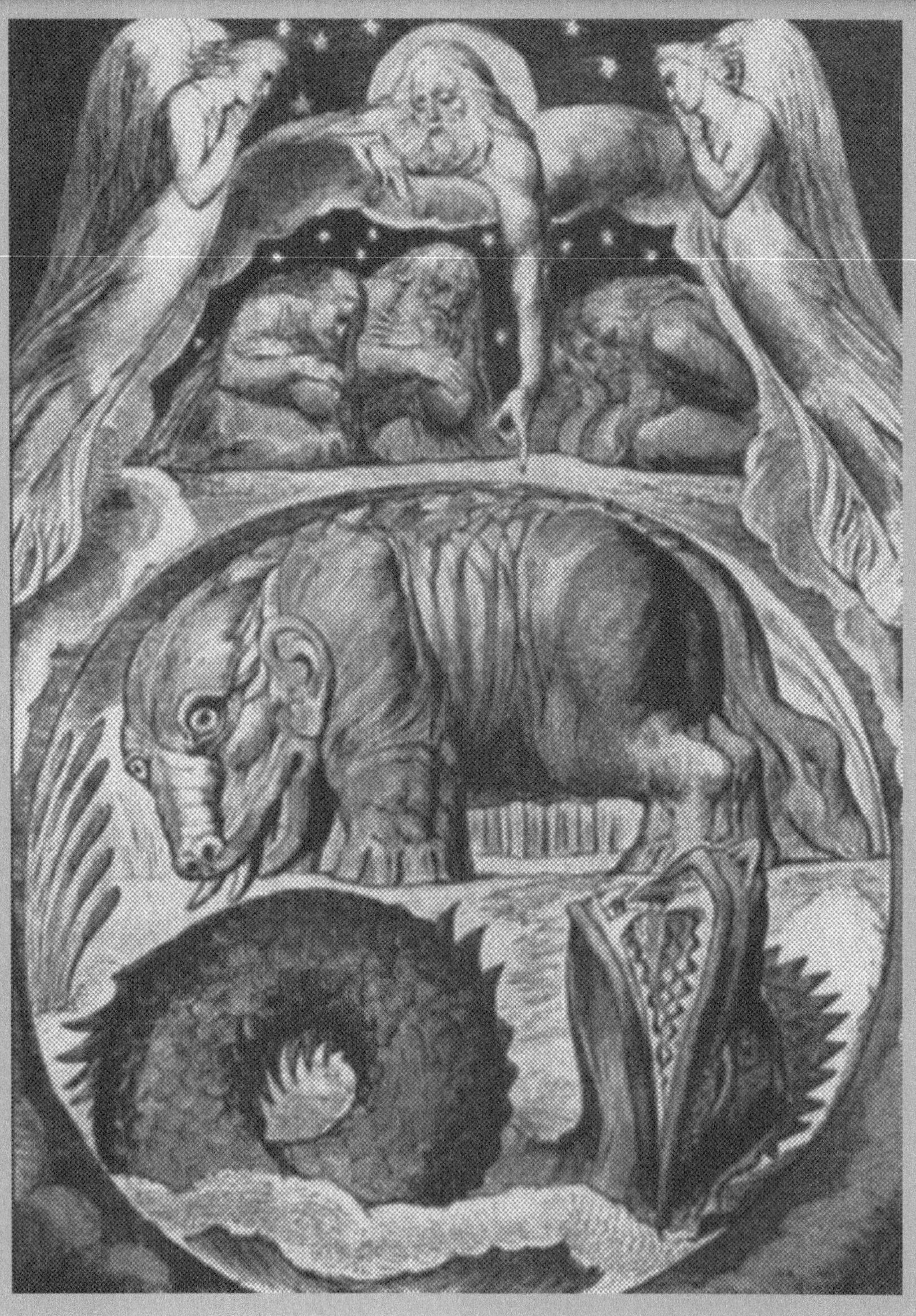

Exploits of Strong Gravity

According to Blake's illustration *Behemoth*, by his helium light, his mind, strong Gravity created all things, energy, mass and light, sun, moon, stars and the atom, noble gas radon. Atom Lambda, the radon Higgs boson in the hindbrain, the cerebellar cortex, maintains and regulates the systems and lights within all people.

Strong Gravity is Atom Lambda, the radon Higgs boson, a carbon copy of the helium Higgs boson, ruler of the central nervous system. Atom Lambda, whose throne is the sun, created and commands all things. Atom Lambda is within every singularity, every new gamete, conception, fertilized zygote that grows into a child. Inside of strong Gravity is Atom Lambda; indeed inside every energy pod, there is the behemoth, the beast, who constitutes "The War occurring within all of us, "the war of all versus all.

At the top, the brain, indeed within the predestined mind, the archetype, is strong Gravity, the mind. The stars are gluon light, the evening stars, each for beauty, with her own separate purpose in the evening sky. Neutron, the weak-electroweak interaction, the archangel Gabriel, is on the left side of strong Gravity. Gluon strong nuclear, the archangel Michael, is on the right side of strong Gravity.

Strong Gravity's arm swinging down by the force of gravity, divides life from death. Below the archangel Michael are the Jewels, heads bowed, bended knee. These three are life: Judah (proton), Israel (gluon) and Jerusalem (neutron). The two holding rocks, fecal matter, their food and urine, their wine, are the quark-antiquark pairs. These came to be when gluon was raped by a photon, who merged with the Z boson, her father, and entered the nucleus of Atom Lambda. The proof is the quark inflationary period that threatened to destroy Atom Lambda altogether. Photon wanted a body for herself, like proton, gluon and neutron. But she is electricity, a random inexplicable killer, Cain, whose anger, in word and deed has destroyed many a good Jewel, Judah, Israel and Jerusalem. Photon did not get the body he wanted, however, the quark, Sardis, sees photon and hears her. She carries electricity and is volatile, in the mood to destroy. The antiquarks carry magnetism. Through photon, they spin large, the impossible, in tiny increments, spin ½. In this way, they are liars, deceivers, taking whatever they want, money including the virginity of women. They are bandits, whose mine field is the innocent Jewels, the naïve, the childlike.

In the stomach is the behemoth, electroweak interaction joined with photon, the transformers, dividing the food by its nutritional value, feeding Atom Lambda in the hindbrain, nourishing the blood. Z boson, the electroweak interaction carrying photon electromagnetism into the womb of life, Atom Lambda, is the root cause of the six quark-antiquark pairs, the invasive six weeds coming up from the bladder and bowels, from photon the serpent, a photon carrying electricity conjoined to a photon carrying magnetism, electromagnetism. The stomach folds into magnetism conjoined together in photon, the serpent below.

The Photon Strangler

1 But there were false prophets [Jerusalem
(neutron with Z boson) and the Gentiles
(quark-antiquark with photon) also among
the people Judah (proton strong Gravity),
Israel (gluon strong nuclear) and Jerusalem
(neutron W^3 boson)], even as there shall be
false teachers among you, who privily [in
whispers] shall bring in damnable heresies
[lies designed to cheat you out of your life],
even denying [Atom Lambda] the Lord that
bought them, and bring upon themselves
swift destruction. 2 And many [Judah, Israel,
Jerusalem and the Gentiles] shall follow
their pernicious ways [sedition]; by reason of
whom the way of truth shall be evil spoken of
[denounced by liars speaking in the mind]. 3
And through covetousness [envy] shall they
with feigned words make merchandise of you
[to be bought and sold in the electromagnetic
field]: whose judgment now of a long time
lingers not, and their damnation slumbers
not.

2 Peter 2:1-3 KJV

The strangler

The Brazil nut is a three-sided nut with white meat, 70 percent fat and 17 percent protein. In physics, it is the Z boson, a photon and the W^3 boson merged as the electroweak interaction of the Special Unitary Group 3. The three children of Atom Lambda are also three sides in one nucleus, proton, gluon and neutron. We are three Jewels, Judah, Israel and Jerusalem.

20 For where two or three are gathered together in my name, there am I in the midst of them. Matthew 18:20 KJV

Like the Jewels, for thousands of years the Brazil nut tree grew, not needing anything, wanting for nothing. GOD, strong Gravity himself protected her, giving her light and water, feeding her and clothing her, giving her special work to improve the world. For the Jewels were his to love and to care for.

Ficus watkinsiana on Syzygium hemilampra-Iluka

Now, the Strangler fig,[1] also called the golden fig, is a large fast-growing tree with a familiar history. It begins its life as a quark, a seed, an epiphyte, a parasite. Borne of birds and monkeys that eat the fig fruit, the seeds are fecal material dropped from the air into the highest branches of this fig tree. The seed lodges in the cracks and crevices of the bark of the host, the Brazil nut tree. The seed germinates and sends out air roots from the top of the tree down some 160 feet into the land. These air roots take in nutrients and water from the air and from host tree. It grows because of the light, the warm sun, which it has never seen as fecal matter buried in the bowels. With time in the life-giving sun, the air roots develop their

1 Found in south Florida and the West Indies.

own underground root system, intermingling its roots with the roots, surrounding the host tree, but independent of it. Once there, the strangler covers the host tree with its own trunk and squeezing out the life and taking it for it's own in a choke hold. It grows quickly and eventually suffocates the host. When the host tree dies, it leaves an enormous upright strangler with a hollow core.

When Eve ate photon's fruit, it grew quickly into a tree, the tree of the knowledge of good and evil. Eventually it would suffocate the Tree of Life in the midst of the garden, the energy den (e-den).

The tree of knowledge is native to coastal areas of every e'phod: the bowels, bladder, stomach, liver, and kidneys.

We recognize that it is true as we may witness the devastation every day in the ill-working digestive tract, the arthritis in your joints, your forgetfulness, your emotional distress.

If the Tree of Life, the central nervous system, were to die right now, it would leave an enormous upright strangler for photon to build her nest. And she has done this in the forebrain. Now, in this age, photon electromagnetism surrounds the hollow shell That is mankind. We would die, but Atom Lambda keeps us alive. For without him there is no life.

Now, there are many problems in the world of mankind. The first of which is the fighting between the children of photon, the Gentiles and the Jewels. Don't pretend that you do not hear the voices in your mind, saying all manner of things, lies.

Now we act like photon and her brood, the Gentiles. Fighting with family, we are constantly at war, in a state of mania. We need to be pitied, held, loved. For the lack of this we weep, nursing our state of depression. We are punished. Where the central nervous system does not respond, the parasympathetic nervous system beefs up and we are beaten to make us stop crying. We die; never having realized why or how we lived.

Mind and Body at War

The mind and the body are at war, as demonstrated by restless leg syndrome, magnetism marching up and down your legs and feet forcing you to move for relief.

The mind says "get up" in the morning but your body is a brick; it won't move. Photon and his brood are no longer diligent in the digestive system. The stomach is in constant turmoil. By the lies you hear in your mind, the what ifs and the electricity surging through your colon, you fear, believing all roads lead to the grave. The don't. Jesus, Atom Lambda Saves. ✍

Photon electromagnetism, Jezebel

The Devil and Satan, Quark-antiquarks, origin of the Gentiles

Aurora Consurgens, Illustrations
15th Century

The quarks carries electricity. To get that feeling of great power he excretes his fecal matter and urine and eats and drink. This is no problem. The quark-antiquark pairs reside in the bowels, the bladder of all who eat. The antiquarks, who carry electromagnetism, eat menstrual blood, a living mass. In the hole where her heart should be, there are living people, protons, gluons and neutrons. Electromagnetism is Ouroboros, the *serpent:* electroweak, electromagnetism and weak force), the dragon eating its own tail. As Saturn, Ouranus, he devours and imprisons his multi-personality children, cyclops.

Fate of Photon

Notwithstanding, I [Jesus Christ Atom Lambda] have a few things against you [Z boson, electroweak force, creator of photon].

Because you suffer [allow] that woman Jezebel [photon electromagnetism], which calls herself a prophetess, to teach [lies] and to seduce my servants [arousing their loins while displaying lewd pictures in their minds] to commit fornication, and to eat things, [fecal matter, urine and menstrual blood] sacrificed to idols: [photons, quark-antiquark pairs or Z bosons].

And I gave her space [time] to repent of her fornication. And she repented not. Behold, I [Atom Lambda] will cast her into a [death] bed. And them [whether Judah, Israel and Jerusalem or the Gentiles] that commit adultery with her [will be cast] into great tribulation [mental, physical, financial, social], except they repent of their deeds.

And I will kill her children [the Gentiles, Sardis and Ephesus] with death [electricity].

And all the churches[1] shall know that I [Jesus Christ Atom Lambda] am he [in the hindbrain] which searches the reins [of the forces (horses) that reside within the living to see where they are being led]. And [I search the] hearts[2] [to see that which is treasured]. And I [Atom Lambda] will give unto every one of you [Z or W3] according to your works.

Revelations 20-20-23 KJV

1 Churches are energy pods with minds that contemplate, voices that speak and arms that perform work and legs and feet that walk

2 For where your treasure is, there will your heart be also. Matthew 6:21 KJV

Who is the Devil and Satan?

That people should fear and abhor her.

The word [magnetism] of the LORD [Jesus Christ Atom Lambda] came to Ezekiel [the electroweak-weak interaction] again, saying, Son of man, say unto [photon electromagnetism] the prince of Tyrus,

This says [Atom Lambda] the Lord GOD: Because your heart [mind] is lifted up [into the forebrain of all people], and you have said, I am [a force], a God. I sit in the seat [the bowels and bladder] of God [strong Gravity], in the midst of the [electromagnetic] seas.

Yet, though you set your heart [desires] as the heart [thoughts and desires] of God [strong Gravity], you are a man [unable to know the whole truth], not God.

Behold, you are wiser than Daniel [neutron Z or W^3 bosons, who questioned Atom Lambda's purpose]. There is no secret that they [Judah, Israel and Jerusalem or the Gentiles] can hide from you. With your wisdom and understanding you have taken riches [stopped neurons from connecting to axons]. And you have gotten gold [proton, Adam] and silver [gluon, Eve] into your treasuries. By your great wisdom [ability to deceive] and your] traffic [magnetism] have you increased your riches [stealing synaptic light before the connect; drawing in the Jewels to serve your purposes]. And your heart [mind] is lifted up [in arrogance] because of your riches.

Therefore, the Lord GOD says this: Because you have set your heart as the heart of God, behold, therefore I will bring strangers [antiquarks carrying magnetism] upon you, the terrible of the nations. [In magnetism] they shall draw their swords [electricity] against the beauty of your wisdom. And they shall defile your brightness.

They shall bring you down to the pit [the bowels, the electromagnetic field], and you shall die the deaths of them [the living] that are slain in the midst of the [electromagnetic] seas [moving along as if alive, but they are walking slowly, without energy, as dead].

Will you yet say before [Atom Lambda], him that slays you, I am God?

But [as a light without a force] you shall be a man, and no God [force], in the hand of him that slays you. You shall die the deaths of the uncircumcised [those carrying electricity, as electricity does not linger, but succumbs swiftly], by the hand of strangers [magnetism]: for I Atom Lambda] have spoken it, says the Lord GOD.

Ezekiel 28:1-10 KJV

Fate of Photon, King of Tyrus

Moreover, [magnetism] the word of [Atom Lambda] the LORD came unto Ezekiel saying, Son of man, take up a lamentation upon the king of Tyrus, and say unto him, this says the Lord GOD: You seal up the sum: full of wisdom [magnetism], and perfect in beauty [electricity].

Blake, Dante Hell: Capaneus the blasphemer
1824-27
The two standing off to the right are the W boson. Photon is surrounded by electricity, lightning strikes. The teeth above are magnetism, his crown and glory. He sits upon fecal waste soaked in urine, the source of his lethal power.

You were in Eden [the original energy den, e'phods], the garden of [strong Gravity] God. Every precious stone [Jewel] was your covering: the sardius [Jerusalem, neutron, Z boson], topaz [Israel, gluon], and the diamond [Judah, proton, Higgs boson], the beryl [Jerusalem, neutron, W^3 bosons], the onyx [Judah, proton, Higgs boson], and the jasper [Israel, gluon], the sapphire [Judah, proton, Higgs boson], the emerald [Jerusalem, neutron, Z boson], and the carbuncle [Jerusalem, neutron, W^3 bosons], and gold [Atom Lambda, the sun in the hindbrain]. [1]

The workmanship of your tabrets [electricity, as a tambourine for beating] and of your pipes [magnetism for speaking] was prepared in you in the day that you were created. You [photon] are [electromagnetism] the anointed cherub that covers; and I [Atom Lambda] have set you so.

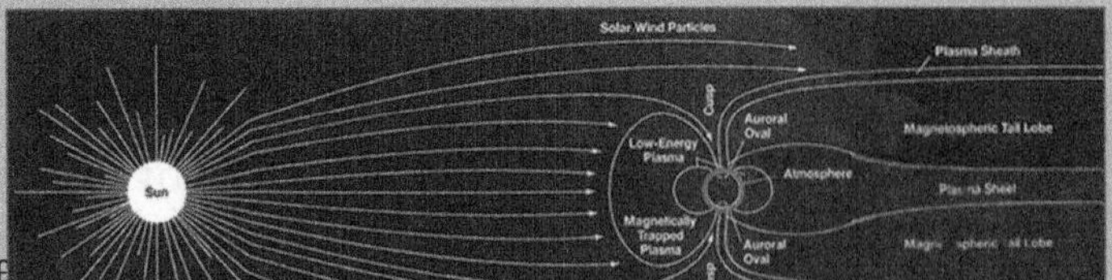

You were upon [the sun] the holy mountain of God [strong Gravity]; you have walked up and down

1 Like gnats generated in dying masses, fruit wastes, photons materialize in fecal waste in atoms, in e'phods.

Photon, the Spectre, Blasphemer, Electromagnetism

in the midst of the [light and mass particles] stones of fire. You were perfect in your ways from the day you were created, till iniquity [evil desires] was found in you; [as demonstrated by Cain, you have a desire to destroy to get rid of your troubles].

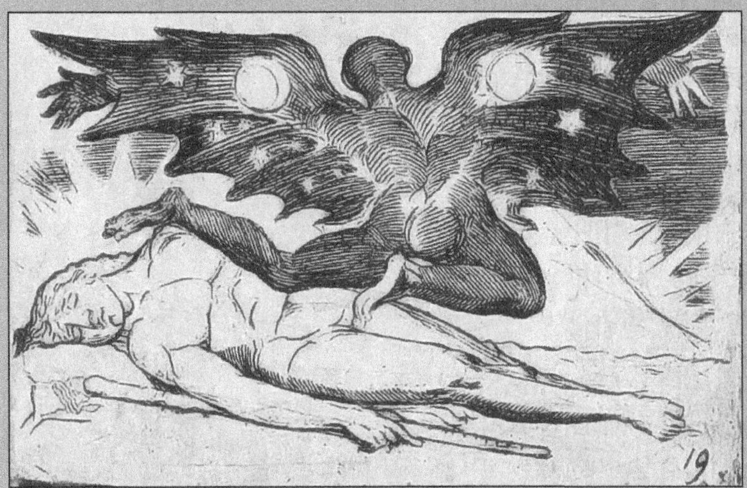

BLAKE, SPECTRE, THE ACCUSER
1821
The spectre is electromagnetism, which is carried by photon. Photon electromagnetism is the anointed cherub that covers mankind, just as magnetism covers the sun.

Merchandise of photon electromagnetism

By the multitude of your merchandise [enticements, magnetism; violence, electricity] they [the Z with W bosons] have filled your midst with violence, and you have sinned. Therefore, I [Atom Lambda] will cast you out of [the forebrain], the mountain of God as profane. And I [Atom Lambda] will destroy you [photon electromagnetism], O covering cherub, from the midst of the stones of fire [atoms, bosons, particles of light, neurons, axons connected to the brain]. Your heart [mind] was lifted up because of your beauty, you have corrupted your wisdom [magnetism] by reason of [electricity] your brightness. I will cast you to the ground [just as photons are cast out of the sun]. I will lay you before kings [all who wear crowns, the crown of the head, so] that they may behold you.

You have defiled your sanctuaries [mass and light, all people] by the multitude of your iniquities [tempting, coercing, deceiving]. Therefore, by the iniquity of your traffic [quarks] will I bring forth a fire from the midst of you [as quarks carry electricity]. It shall devour you. And I will bring you to ashes upon the earth in the sight of all them that behold you [atoms, particles of light]. All they that know you among the people shall be astonished at you. You shall be a terror, and never shall you be any more [in his present form. (Law of conservation)].

Ezekiel 28:11-19 KJV

End of the Age

[This message from Paul and Timothy is written to the saints [Jewels: Judah (proton), Israel (gluon) and Jerusalem (neutron). And it is written to the Gentiles: Sardis (a quark) and Ephesus (an antiquark), the faithful brethren in Christ which are at Colosse:[1]

Grace be to you [who are alive at the end of this age, the age of the Gentiles], and peace, from [strong Gravity] God our Father and [from Atom Lambda] the Lord Jesus Christ. We give thanks to God [strong Gravity], and [Atom Lambda] the Father of [Jesus], our Lord Jesus Christ. [We] pray always for you since we heard of your faith in Christ Jesus, and of the love which you have for all the saints. [We pray] for the hope [understanding], which is laid up for you in heaven [your brain, your minds, your thoughts], of which you [have] heard before in the word of the truth of the gospel. Now, this truth of the gospel has come to you, as it is [known] in all the world [within every atom and is written in the scientific laws]. [This same truth] brings forth fruit [knowledge, understanding and wisdom], as it does also in you since the day you heard of it, and knew [charity], the grace of God in truth.

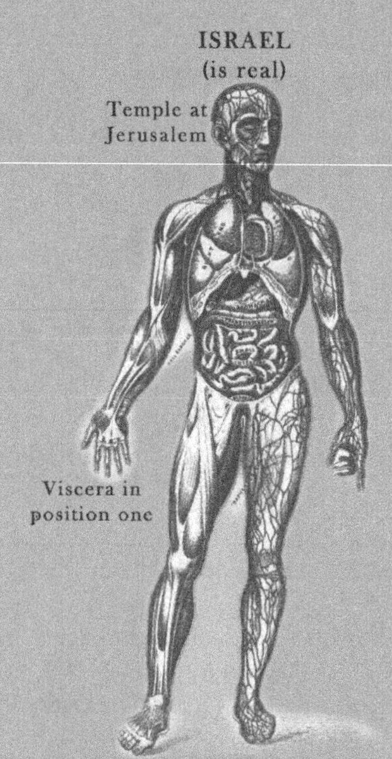

From Energy Den to Energy Pod

[And] you also learned of Epaphras [also known as Ephesus the Gentiles], our dear fellow servant. For you [that are living at the end of this age, Ephesus] is [an example of] a faithful minister of Christ [caring ritualistically for the e'phod, cleansing and eating healthy foods, studying the word and praying diligently]. [It is he] who also declared to us [Paul and Timothy] your love [of Jesus Christ], in [strong Gravity] the Spirit, [that resides within every DNA oxygenated person, the Adam and the atom].

For this cause [faithfulness], since the day we heard it, we also do not cease to pray for you, to desire that you might be filled with the knowledge of his [Atom Lambda's] will: in all wisdom and spiritual understanding [so] that you might walk worthy of [Atom Lambda] the Lord to all pleasing. [In this way] being fruitful in every good work, increasing in the

1 Colosse is a comparative qualifier: The earth (the planet) is colosse compared to an e'phod (a person); an e'phod is colossal compared to an atom..

Atom Lambda, Image of the Invisible God

knowledge of God, strengthened with all might according to his [Atom Lambda's] glorious power, unto all patience and longsuffering with joyfulness.

Giving thanks to [Atom Lambda strong Gravity] the Father, which has made us meet to be partakers of the inheritance of the saints in light [bosons and gluons]. [Atom Lambda strong Gravity] has delivered us from [photon electromagnetism] the power of darkness, and has translated us [from the electromagnetic field] into [the gravitational field] the kingdom of [Atom Lambda] his [strong Gravity's] dear Son. [Atom Lambda is he] in whom we have redemption through his blood [infused within our blood for the repair and restoration of our DNA, freeing us from generational diseases], even the forgiveness of sins [our time without Christ, remanded to the electromagnetic field, doing abominable things, murder, lust, violence].

Who is the image of the invisible God [strong Gravity]; the firstborn of every creature? For by him [Atom Lambda] were all things created that are in heaven [the brain, the mind], and that are in earth [atoms and e'phods]; visible [mass and light] and invisible [forces]. Whether they are thrones [for the ruler of the central nervous system, the hindbrain], or dominions [where bosons rule], or principalities [the bladder and bowels where photon rules], or powers: all things were created by him, and for him. And he [Atom Lambda] is before all things. And by him [Atom Lambda] all things consist [of atoms]. And he [Atom Lambda] is the head of the body [the e'phod, energy pod], the church. [And it is he] who is the beginning [of life as we know it]. [As Jesus Christ, he is] the firstborn from the dead, [so] that in all things he [Atom Lambda] might have the preeminence. For it pleased the Father [strong Gravity] that in him [Atom Lambda] should all fullness [atoms, the composition of all things] dwell. And, having made peace through the blood [desires] of his cross [e'phod, energy pod], by him to reconcile all things unto himself. [For] by him [Atom Lambda], I say, whether they are things in earth [the energy pod], or things in heaven [the mind].

Manic Depression, the Mystery of the Gentiles

And you [Gentiles, having dual minds with conflicting thoughts conjoined in one brain], that were sometimes alienated [as electricity] and enemies [as magnetism, fight against each other purposes] in your mind; [you are haunted] by [your innate] wicked works [, yet now has he [Atom Lambda] reconciled In the body of his flesh through death, to present you holy, blameless, not to be reproved for the past] in his sight [for Atom Lambda is the root cause of all things, sees all things, understands all things; he is us].

Colossians 1:2-22 KJV

Crystallization of Atom Lambda
Birth of Jesus Christ

> "The book of the generation of Jesus Christ, Atom Lambda, the son of David, gluon strong nuclear; the son of Abraham, neutron, who has three lights. Abraham as neutron begat Isaac, proton strong Gravity; and Isaac, proton, begat Jacob, gluon strong nuclear; and Jacob begat Judas and his brethren, the quark-antiquark pairs and the Gentiles, children of photon electromagnetism, who raped gluon to conceive them.
>
> Matthew 1:1-2 KJV

Mary, Joseph and Jesus

Now the birth of Jesus Christ[1] was on this wise: When as his mother Mary [the Z boson or W3] was espoused to Joseph [Israel, gluon strong nuclear], before they came together, she was found [pregnant] with child of [strong Gravity], the Holy Ghost. Then Joseph her husband, being a just man, and not willing to make her a public example, was minded to put her away privily. But while he thought on these things, behold, [Michael, a gluon] the angel of the Lord [Atom Lambda] appeared unto him in a dream, saying, Joseph, son of David [Israel, gluon strong nuclear], fear not to take to yourself Mary [as] your wife: for that which is conceived in her is [a proton gamete] of the Holy Ghost [strong Gravity, a seed in the image of Atom Lambda]. And she shall bring forth a son [Atom Lambda, as a babe, in an ephod]; and you shall call his name JESUS]: For he shall save his people [within whom he resides] from their sins [electromagnetic infections in the mind and body].

The Prophecy

Now all this was done [so] that it might be fulfilled [that] which was spoken of the Lord [Atom Lambda] by the prophet, saying, Behold, a virgin shall be with child, and shall bring forth a son, and they shall call his name Emmanuel, which being interpreted is, God with us [in the hindbrain of every living person]. Then Joseph, being raised from sleep, did as the angel of the Lord had bidden him, and took [Mary] unto him [as] his wife: And [Joseph] knew her not till she had brought forth her firstborn son. And he called his name JESUS: [A homograph: He's Us; Atom Lambda lives within us and we live within him.]

Matthew 1:18-25 KJV

---

1 Jesus Christ is proton, strong Gravity crystallized, lit by the Higgs boson. He is a carbon copy of Atom Lambda who rules the earth from the sun. According to the Law of Conservation, energy, mass and light changes forms. From before spacetime strong Gravity has always existed. From period one, hydrogen and the noble gas helium, strong Gravity crystallized.

Photon, Herod
Three Wise Men

Three Wise Men

Now when Jesus was born in Bethlehem [the uterus, a city of synaptic lights, bosons and particles forming and conforming] in Judaea [the reproductive system]. In the days of Herod the king [the Gentiles, like Cain, made in the image of photon electromagnetism], behold, there came wise men [Jewels: Judah (proton], Israel [gluon] and Jerusalem (neutron)] from the east [the midbrain], to Jerusalem [the hindbrain], saying, Where is he that is born King of the Jews [the Jewels, particles of mass and light, people], the foundation stones? For we have seen his star in the east, and are come to worship him. When Herod the king [photon] had heard these things, he was troubled, and all Jerusalem [those living in the city of Jerusalem] with him. And when he had gathered all the chief priests and scribes of the people together, he demanded of them where Christ should be born. And they said unto him, In Bethlehem of Judaea: for thus it is written by the prophet, and you Bethlehem [the city], in the land of Judah [atoms], are not the least among the princes of Judah: for out of you shall come a Governor that shall rule my people Israel [the three Jewels born of David].

Then Herod, when he had privily called the wise men [as deceivers do], he enquired of them diligently what time the star appeared. And he sent them to Bethlehem, and said, Go and search diligently for the young child; and when you have found him, bring me word again, that I may come and worship him also. When they had heard the king, they departed; and, lo, the [gluon] star, which they saw in the east [over the midbrain], went before them till it came and stood over where the young child was. When they saw the star, they rejoiced with exceeding great joy. And when they were come into the house, they saw [proton Atom Lambda, strong Gravity], the [rudiments of the] young child with Mary [the weak interaction], his mother, and fell down, and worshiped him. And when they had opened their treasures, they presented unto him gifts; [proton gave] gold (synaptic gold, understanding]; [and gluon gave] frankincense [autoimmunity for healing body and mind], and [neutron provided] myrrh [bitterness for learning, growing wise].

Matthew 2:1-11 KJV

Radon, Period seven, the Seventh Day of Creation

Thus the heavens [energy and light] and the earth [elemental atoms] were finished, and all the host of them. And on the seventh day [Atom Lambda] God [strong Gravity] ended his work [the six periods that produced the six noble gases] which he had made.

And he [Atom Lambda] rested on the seventh day [period seven on the periodic table of the elements] from all his work which he had made, [as the six noble gases were completed]. And God [Atom Lambda, strong Gravity] blessed the seventh day [the seventh light, the radon Higgs boson, whose mass is Atom Lambda, residing in the hindbrain of every person]. And [strong Gravity] sanctified it [the seventh day, period]. Because in it [the seventh period of the elements] he [Atom Lambda who rules from the sun] had rested from all his work which God [strong Gravity] created and made.

Genesis 2:1-3 KJV

Generations of Mass and Life

These are the generations of the heavens [the minds of people] and of the earth [atoms, Eden, the energy dens] when they were created; in the day that [Atom Lambda] the LORD God, made the earth [hydrogen mass, atoms] and the heavens [the noble gases that light the mind]: and every plant [eukaryotes: Judah (proton) and Israel (gluon); and Jerusalem (neutron) the archaic being] of the [gravitational] field before it was in the earth [in atoms comprising walking energy pods, communicating with Atom Lambda and each other]. And every [prokaryote, quark-antiquark pair, the Gentiles, the] herb of the [electromagnetic] field before it grew [into living beings].

For [while Adam was acquiring mass, organ by organ and system by system], [Atom Lambda] the LORD God had not caused it to rain upon the earth [hydrogen mass, atoms]: and there was not a man to till the ground: [the man is a copy of Atom Lambda in the sun that rules the sympathetic nervous system from the hind brain].[1] But there went up a mist from [magnetism, within the masses]; and [by the moisture within the force that puts out fires, magnetism] watered the whole face of the ground [atom by atom within Adam]. And [Atom Lambda] the LORD God formed man [from Atom Lambda to Adam] of the dust [atoms] of the ground; and [Atom Lambda] breathed into his nostrils the breath of life; and man became a living soul [a boson, a light lit by a noble gas].[2]

And the LORD God planted a garden [ruled by Michael, gluon strong nuclear] eastward in Eden [where all movement, reactions and understanding, the inferior olive nucleus]; and there he put the [light, lit by a noble gas, the mind of the] man [Adam] whom he had formed.

And out of the ground [atoms, of which the man was formed], the LORD God made to grow every tree [that of DNA and RNA] that is pleasant to the sight, and [protons, gluons and neutrons with elemental atoms that are] good for food. [Atom Lambda, in the sun, also placed the radon Higgs boson lit by the noble gas radon created on the sixth day], the tree of life, also in the midst of the garden [in the brain]: and the tree of knowledge of good and evil [quark-antiquark pairs of the bladder and bowels].

Genesis 2:4-9 KJV

Strong Gravity, the River of Life

And a [hydrogen] river went out of Eden to water the garden; and from thence it was parted, and became into four heads.

Genesis 2:10 KJV

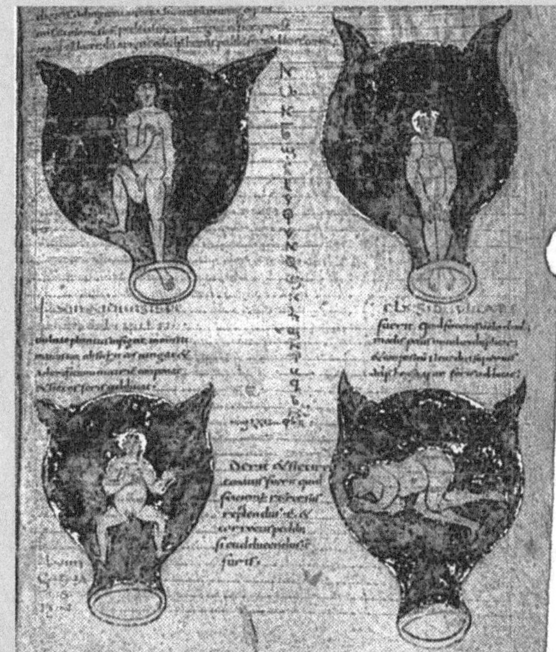

BRUSSELS KONINKLIJKE BIBLIOTHEEK VAN BELGIE, Bibliothèque royale de Belgique ms. 3701-15 58

Left to right, top to bottom, Adam is Pison, strong Gravity. Beside strong Gravity is the weak-electroweak force, pious. Below strong Gravity is gluon strong nuclear, the mass maker, lover, child bearer, healer. Gluon is light, like the Higgs boson and is mass like proton, within a single being. The fourth river, Euphrates, ends at the bowels and bladder. She waits to be taken by mankind, her lovers. We are each one of these four, our minds lit as the rivers are lit, by five of the six noble gases.

The name of the first [river] is Pison [pis-on, as hydrogen flows downward from Atom Lambda by the force of gravity]: that is it which encompasses the whole land of Havilah [have-a-lot], where there is gold [Atom Lambda, whose light is the golden light lit with helium, of the sun]; And the gold of that land is good [perceptive, intuitive, with understanding]: there is bdellium [electricity] and the onyx stone [magnetism, strong Gravity's coupling constant].

And the name of the second river is Gihon [gluon strong nuclear, Ourania, of the gravitational field]. Like Eve is Adam's helpmate, gluon is Atom Lambda's helper, hands and feet]: [This gluon, Pandemos], is the same [mass and light] that encompasses the whole land of Ethiopia [the mass of the electromagnetic field].

And the name of the third river is Hiddekel [hidden intentions]: that is it which goes toward the east [toward the forebrain] of Assyria [the bladder and bowels]. And [within the third river] the fourth river is Euphrates [the toxic photon electromagnetism, which follows the digestive system from salivation within the mouth, the drainage of the sinus cavities to the bladder and bowels through excretion].

Genesis 2:11-14 KJV

War of All Versus All

The war of all versus all is occurring right now within the body, the ephod or energy pod, previously known as Eden or Adam's energy den before the creation of Eve. The war of all versus is also occurring within the mind, and between people: mankind and humankind, Jewels versus the Gentiles, every family; crystalline antibodies versus liquefying quark-antiquark bodies. The evidence is disease, pain, bad news where you can't get a break, stress.

Leonardo da Vinci, Battle of Anghiari
1505
The war between the four universal forces and lights (the clash of the titans, is occurring within every person and between people.

1 Woe is me! For I am as when they have gathered the summer fruits, as the grape
gleanings of the vintage: there is no cluster to eat: my soul desired the first ripe fruit. 2
The good man is perished out of the earth: And there is none upright among men: they
all lie in wait for blood; They hunt, every man, his brother with a net.

3 That <u>they</u> [Sardis and Ephesus as photon with Z boson] may do evil with both
hands earnestly; the <u>prince</u> [Israel gluon strong nuclear] <u>asks</u> [and receives favors]; and
the <u>judge</u> [Jerusalem Z or W^3 boson] <u>asks for a reward</u> [extorts]; and the <u>great man</u>
[Judah strong Gravity], he utters his mischievous desire: so they wrap it up.

4 The best of <u>them</u> [of mankind] is as a brier: the <u>most upright</u> [of the humankind]
is sharper than a thorn hedge: The day of your <u>watchmen</u> [Jerusalem (SU(3)]and your
visitation comes: Now shall be their perplexity.

5 Trust you not in a friend, put not your confidence in a guide: keep the doors of
your mouth from [photon] <u>her</u> that lies in your bosom.

6 For the son dishonours the father, the daughter rises up against her mother, the
daughter in law against her mother in law; a man's enemies are the men of his own
house. 7 Therefore I will look unto the LORD; I will wait for the God of my salvation:
my God will hear me.

Micah 7:1-7 KJV

No Peace for this Age

34 Think not that I am come to send peace on earth: I came not to send peace, but a sword [Israel
gluon strong nuclear, David]. 35 For I am come to set a man at variance against his father, and
the daughter against her mother, and the daughter in law against her mother in law. 36 And a
man's foes shall be [his children, the Gentiles], they of his own household.

37 He that loves father or mother more than me is not worthy of me: and he that loves [Cain,
his Gentiles] son or daughter, more than me is not worthy of me. 38 And he that taketh not his
cross [his energy pod], and follows after me, is not worthy of me. 39 He that finds his life shall
lose it: and he that loses his life *for my sake* shall find it. 40 He that receives you receives me, and
he that receives me receives him that sent me.

Matthew 10:34-40 KJV

Atom Lambda, Christ

1. Strong Gravity crystallized as hydrogen, creator of all things universal and local, the living and the dead ones who move within and among us upon the earth.
2. From proton came gluon, crystalline DNA and RNA, the healer, ruler of the immunological armies.
3. From proton came helium, the sun, the light that is the eye of Atom Lambda.
4. He was called LORD or LORD God, but his name is Atom Lambda. He is the first hydrogen atom, protium 1H.
5. Requires nothing but provides everything for life. As strong Gravity, Atom Lambda speaks to us and through us. (Luke 12:12 KJV)
6. Feeds the sympathetic nervous system with fire, synaptic light.
7. Provides truth to those that will hear.
8. As strong Gravity, Atom Lambda, a proton, has three children called mankind. They are named in the scriptures as Judah (proton 1H), Israel (gluon, (proton 2H) and Jerusalem (neutron, (proton 3H).
9. Atom Lambda consumes elemental nutrients of the first fruits every time the living consumes food and drink.

Photon, Antichrist

1. Photon liquefies mass in energy pods of the living and after death.
2. Photon poisonous in nature. From gallium to germanium, arsenic, selenium, bromine to krypton, the energy releaser, chaos.
3. Photon is death, electricity, a mania for destruction or sudden death; and the grave, magnetism, depression.
4. Photon is the light bearer, not the light, Atom Lambda. Photon is Bar-Jesus, *not Jesus*, though he presents himself as God. He is a deceiver, chaos, confusion.
5. Photon gives wings to any that will accept them to fly into a rage and destroy or to plunge into intense weeping. Photon's wings, electromagnetism, are the source of man's pride, violence.
6. Photon is responsible for waste management in every living creature, moving waste from the large intestine outside of the body.
7. Because of photon, there are six types of quark-antiquark pairs, instruments of death, evidence of the rape of gluon before the world was made. They make the rocks in the large intestines, molding liquid waste into solid waste, sand castles. Like pigs, they eat the fecal matter (bread) and drink urine (wine), as they work.

Original Sin

MICHELANGELO, ORIGINAL SIN
1508-1512

Holding photon's hand, Eve ate from the tree of the knowledge of good and evil, semen that conveys fecal matter and urine, discarded blood wastes, elements found in DNA. Many people are consuming wastes from the bladder and bowels today for pleasure, euphoria, joining themselves to photon; making him their master. And Atom Lambda, life, is usurped in favor of anticipated pleasures proposed by photon, who pushes us to experience death while we yet live.

15 And [Atom Lambda] the LORD God took [the radon Higgs boson, Atom Lambda, ruler of the central nervous system], the man, and put him into the garden of Eden [e-den, Adam's energy den] to dress it [with knowledge and with clothing] and to keep it [healthy, productive and wise].

16 And [Atom Lambda] the LORD God commanded the man [Atom Lambda in the hindbrain], saying, Of every tree [mass: protons, gluons and neutrons] of the garden [e'phod, energy phod], you may freely eat:

17 But of [the bladder and bowels], the tree [where quark-antiquark masses, who consume fecal matter and urine to exist, are ruled by photon], of the knowledge of good [life in the gravitational field] and evil [dying and death in the electromagnetic field], you shall not eat of it.

For in the day that you eat thereof, you shall surely die; [for your soul will convert from the gravitational field - life into the electromagnetic field - where you will exist as the dead].

Genesis 2:15-17 KJV

[As the energy, mass and light within you begins to fail without notice and the immunological armies wait for the command from Atom Lambda that does not come. The mass gives way to inflammation, disease, loss of energy. The mind relents to loss of understanding and loss of memory, as these are provided by Atom Lambda, which, once you eat that bread – fecal matter and drink that wine – urine and eat that fruit – sperm.]

Essentials of Mankind, the Lights

Sandro Botticelli, Birth of Venus
1485–1486

The birth of Venus is the birth of gluon strong nuclear, as Jacob. Venus is made by Atom Lambda who is carried by strong Gravity. She was placed in a shell while she grew, acquiring, power, light. Jealous like Esau, the electroweak interaction holds a cloth ready to cover up her light, her beauty.

A Helper for Atom Lambda in the Hindbrain

18 And [Atom Lambda] the LORD God said, It is not good that the man [whose central nervous system is ruled by the Higgs boson][1] should be alone; I will make him a help meet [gluon strong nuclear][2] for him.

19 And out of [atoms] the ground [Atom Lambda] the LORD God formed every beast[3] of the [gravitational] field, and every [flying] fowl [boson, gluon, photon] of the air; and brought them unto Adam to see what he would call them: and whatsoever [scientific name] Adam [Judah] called every living creature, that was the name thereof.

20 And Adam [Judah] gave names to all cattle [neutrons], and to the fowl of the air, and to every beast of the [gravitational] field; but for Adam there was not found an help meet [support and defense] for him.

Genesis 2:18-20 KJV

1 The Higgs boson commands the forces, and conveys mass and light upon a body.
2 Gluon strong nuclear rules the midbrain and carries out the commands of Atom Lambda; for Atom Lambda is stationary in the cerebellar cortex, like Atom Lambda, who emanates the light of the sun.
3 A beast is a composition of life consisting of energy, mass and light.

Creation of Eve

Michelangelo, Creation of Eve
1508-1512

Eve is taken from Adam's deoxyRIBonucleic acid (DNA) by Atom Lambda. Strong Gravity is the ignudi at the top, chaste. Below strong Gravity is the strong nuclear interaction, scratching his head as if to say, Hum. Beside strong nuclear is the electroweak interaction, open to anything. Above him is electromagnetism, whose green cloak is magnetism expelling electricity randomly.

Creation of Eve

21 And [Atom Lambda] the *LORD God* caused a deep sleep to fall upon Adam, and he
slept: and he took one of his *ribs* [his deoxyRIBonucleic acid, DNA], and closed up the
flesh instead thereof; 22 And the rib, which the LORD God had taken from man, made
he a woman, and brought her unto the man.

23 And Adam said, This is now bone of my bones, and flesh of my flesh:

She shall be called Woman, because she was taken out of Man.

24 Therefore shall a man leave his father and his mother, and shall cleave unto his
wife [the radon Higgs boson]: and they shall be one flesh.

25 And *they* [the light that lights the mind of the child and the light that is the radon
Higgs boson, Atom Lambda] *were both naked*, the man [a Higgs boson] and his *wife* [a
gluon], and were not ashamed.

Genesis 2:21-25 KJV

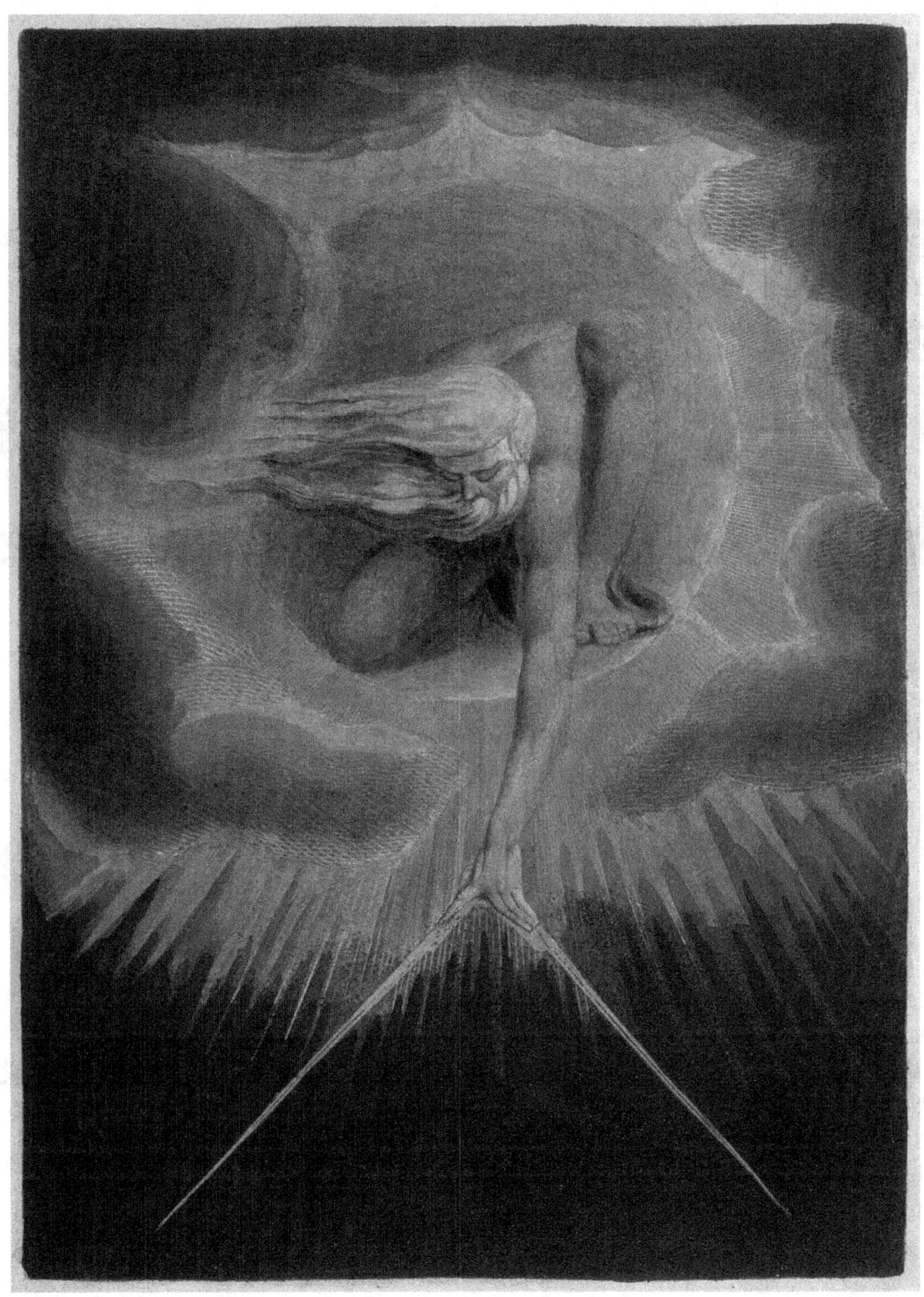

BENTLEY, ERDMAN, KEYNES, Europe a Prophecy, British Museum
1794

Atom Lambda in the sun has a yokes on each of us. It is the Z boson, electricity and the three W bosons of magnetism. The Z boson also calls upon photon, an agent of death, electromagnetism, to cause a change of inclination in the mind and changes to all flesh, itching, burning and flaking skin and sudden attacks of electricity and hardly noticeable pain, the humming of magnetism.

Original Sin

"1 Now [Z, photon, W^3 boson] the serpent, was more subtil than any beast of the [electromagnetic] field, which [Atom Lambda] the LORD God] had made. And he said to [Eve] the woman, Yea, has God said, You shall not eat of *every* tree of the garden? 2 And the woman said to the serpent, We may eat of the fruit of the trees of the garden: 3 But of [fecal matter, blood wastes and urine] the fruit of the tree [the reproductive, waste removal system], which is in the midst of the garden [the energy den], God has said, You shall not eat of it, neither shall you touch it [the toxic waste], lest you [your soul] die.

Genesis 3:1-3 KJV

Photon wants a body, a child (like Jesus, born of a woman)

And the serpent said unto the woman, You shall not surely die. 5 For God does know that in the day you eat thereof [of the fruit excreted from the bladder and bowels], then your eyes shall be opened, and you shall be as gods [forces], knowing good [strong Gravity] and evil [electromagnetism].

Classic Misdirection

6 And when the woman saw that the tree [that culminates in the reproductive organs] was good for food, and that it was pleasant to the eyes [bosons, pleasure for the soul], and a tree [for learning] to be desired, to make one wise, she took of the fruit [fecal and blood wastes, and urine] thereof [excreted from the reproductive organs], and did eat [semen knitted by quark-antiquark pairs, mucus]. And gave also unto [Atom Lambda in the hindbrain] her husband with [in] her; and he did eat [the toxicity and died, leaving the central nervous system unattended].[1] 7And the eyes of them both were opened, and they knew that they were naked [true, is real]. And they sewed [justifications as] fig leaves [deception upon deception] together, and made themselves

Blake, The Serpent in the E'Phod
1825-1827

Above, in the house, the brain, mind in the gravitational field, there is Mary (neutron) the mother, Joseph (gluon) the father and Jesus Christ, an e'phod for Atom Lambda. The serpent is made for waste management, the bladder and bowels and resides with his charges in the electromagnetic field, moving back and forth into the gravitational field. Alas, photon has drawn the minds of many Jewels into the electromagnetic field to seek pleasure, to eat waste from the bladder and bowels.

---

1 When Atom Lambda in the hindbrain is not ruling the central nervous system, it is open to thieves, vultures. Photon rules the body and mind applying the consequences of the parasympathetic nervous system, causing ailments, loss of energy. As photon does not command the forces; only Atom Lambda can.

MICHELANGELO, SIN OF EVE
1508-1512
The serpent is a photon, electromagnetism, is part of a system of lights, formed by the Z boson. The third light in the serpent system is the W bosons, 3 lights that rotates in one. As all people carry the force of magnetism. Like Atom Lambda, photon speaks to us, in our thoughts. She knows our desires. If we eat her fruit, photon becomes ruler of many curious minds and bodies, causing people to behave violently or weep without understanding.

aprons [to hide the truth and to justify their actions].

Adam and Eve Exposed

8 And they heard [Atom Lambda] the voice of [strong Gravity] the LORD God walking [propelled by gluon strong nuclear] in the garden in the cool of the day [evening]. And Adam and [Atom Lambda (hindbrain)], his wife, hid themselves [camouflage, in deceptions that they reasoned together with photon electromagnetism], from the presence of the LORD God, among the trees [anatomical systems] of the garden.

9 And the LORD God called to Adam,
and said to him, Where are you? 10 And he
[Adam] said, I heard [magnetism, speaking with the crackling sound of electricity], your voice in the garden, and I was afraid, because I was naked [exposed, naïve, easily tricked]. And I hid myself.

11 And he [Atom Lambda] said, Who told you that you were naked [naïve, easily tricked]? Have you eaten of the tree, whereof I commanded you that you *should not eat*?

12 And the man said, The woman, whom you gave to be with me, she gave me of the tree and I did eat.

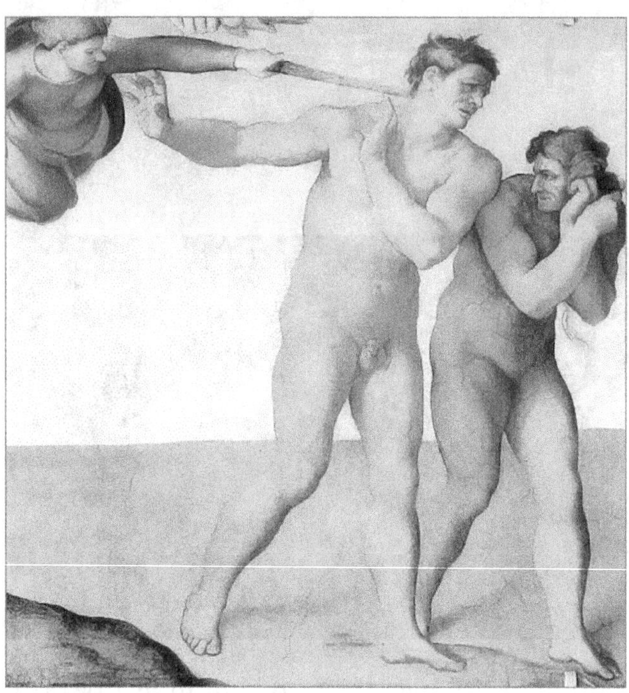

MICHELANGELO, EXPULSION
1508-1512
The angel, electroweak interaction carries a stick, the Z boson with electricity, for shock and awe, for remembrance; and to forget. He points to Atom Lambda, the Higgs boson, in Adam's hindbrain.

13 And the LORD God said unto the woman, What is this that you have done? And the woman said, The serpent [electroweak, electromagnetism with weak force] beguiled me, and I did eat.

CURSES, INNATE BEHAVIOURS

THE SERPENT

14 And the LORD God said unto the serpent, Because you have done this, you are cursed above all cattle [neutrons, beasts of burden], and above every beast [energy, mass, light configurations, Judah and Israel] of the [gravitational] field. Upon [Z boson, the light within] your belly shall you go. And dust [protons, gluons and neutrons] shall
you eat all the days of thy life. 15 And I will
put enmity [ill will, animosity] between you and the woman;[2] and between your seed [W^3 boson weak interaction] and her seed [the photon electromagnetism]. It [this demeaning relationship] shall bruise your head [ego], and you shall bruise his heel [expose his weaknesses, in spite of overall strength, causing him to fall].

THE WOMAN

16 Unto the woman he said, I will greatly multiply your sorrow [magnetism with weeping] and your conception [as the Gentiles[3] are, everyone, a twin]. In sorrow, you shall bring forth children. And your desire shall be to your husband [Atom Lambda in the hindbrain, whatever his light tells you to do]. And he Atom Lambda in the hindbrain] shall rule over you [through synaptic activity, neurons, axons].

ADAM AND HIS WIFE IN THE HINDBRAIN

17 And unto Adam he said, Because [in your compassion] you have hearkened to [magnetism] the voice of your wife [in the hindbrain], and have eaten of the tree [the reproductive system] of which I commanded you, saying, Thou shalt not eat of it, cursed is the ground [the hydrogen atom in the hindbrain and its proton mass and Higgs boson light] for your sake [so Judah will learn].[4]

2 Esau and Jacob; Saul and David

3 Cain (electricity) and Able (magnetism) are conjoined minds in a single body.

4 Adam is Judah, the last of creation. So the last (Judah) shall be first and the first (Jerusalem Z or W^3 boson) will be last. Matthew 20:16

In sorrow [depression, magnetism] you shall eat of it [take lessons from Jerusalem W3 the teacher; take discipline from Jerusalem Z boson] all the days of your life. 18 Thorns [photons] also [will taunt you], and with thistles [magnetism] shall it [photon] bring forth [electricity] to you.

And [in your naiveté] you shall eat the herb [follow the opinions, suggestions of neutrons, Jerusalem, the teacher, disciplinarian] of the [gravitational] field.

19 In the sweat of your face [hard work] shall you eat bread [food], till you return to the ground [the hydrogen mass, in death, as light, back to Atom Lambda in the sun]. For out of it [the hydrogen mass] were you taken. For you are dust [proton], and to dust [proton lit by the Higgs boson] you shall return.

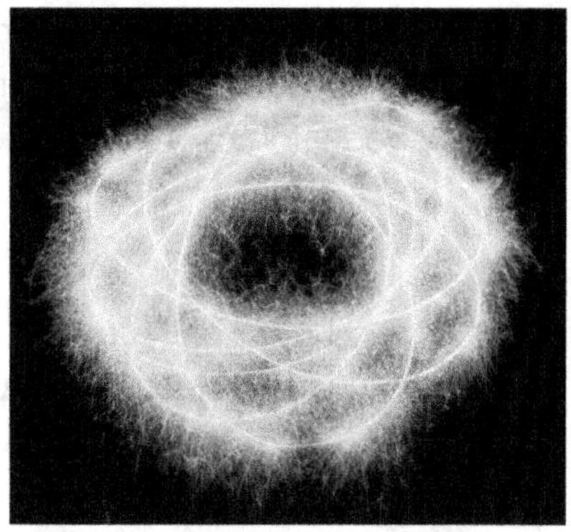

Electrons surrounding the nucleus of an atom, the flaming sword,

Adam's Physical Wife

20 And Adam called his wife's name Eve [by the multitude of the evening stars, all gluon mass as light]. [And] because she was the mother of all living [Judah, Israel and Jerusalem and Ephesus conjoined with Sardis in DNA (but not in RNA].

Fortification of the Spirit

21 Unto Adam [strong Gravity] also and to his wife [Eve, gluon strong nuclear] did [Atom Lambda] the LORD God make coats of skins [layers of resiliency, endurance, with understanding and patience], and [he] clothed them [in fortitude to resist temptation when being tested by the teachers, judges].

22 And the LORD God said, Behold, the man [Adam (Atom Lambda in the hindbrain)] is become as one of us, to know good [life, light, [knowledge, understanding and wisdom] and evil [enslavement, death, darkness]. And now, [he is banished from Eden, energy den, the atom], lest he put forth [gluon] his hand and take also of the tree of life [proton, the hydrogen atom in the sun], and eat, and live for ever.

23 Therefore the LORD God sent him forth from the garden of Eden, to till the ground [as a scientist, to investigate, research, analyze and understand] from where he was taken.

24 So he drove out the man. And he placed at the east of the garden of Eden,[5] cherubims [Z bosons] and a flaming sword [electrons] which turned every way, to keep the way of the tree of life.

Genesis 3:1-24 KJV

5 Atom Lambda is the energy den, the sanctuary, where forces and light enter and leave the atom. Adam and Eve are lights: a Higgs boson and gluon. By the lights, the forces are summoned to do their work. Both the good works of the gravitational field and the evil works emanating from the electromagnetic field are commanded by Atom Lambda; and the living are in his debt. The same Atom Lambda that brings joy also brings pain. He commands all things: forces, mass, light and people.

Talents, Abilities for Jewels

14 For the kingdom of heaven [the brain, thoughts in the mind] is as a man [Atom Lambda] traveling into a far country [to explore the gravitational field and its adjunct the electromagnetic field]. [He] called his own [three] servants [Judah, Israel and Jerusalem], and delivered to them his goods [forces, each with special abilities, talents].

JUDAH (HIGGS BOSON)

15 And unto one [Judah] he gave five talents [abilities, forces to command: strong Gravity, strong nuclear, electroweak or weak and magnetism].

ISRAEL (GLUON)

To another [Atom Lambda gave] two [abilities, forces: strong nuclear (a subset of strong Gravity) and electricity].

JERUSALEM (Z BOSON)

And to another [Atom Lambda gave] one [ability, one force: the electroweak interaction].

[Atom Lambda gave] to every man according to his several ability. And [Atom Lambda] straightway took his journey [to explore the far off country within strong Gravity that is the electromagnetic field, death].

JUDAH (PROTON)

16 Then he that had received the five talents went and traded with the same, and made them [Judah and Atom Lambda his wife, who rules from the hindbrain] another five talents.

ISRAEL (GLUON)

17 And likewise, he that had received two [talents], he also gained other two.

JERUSALEM (NEUTRON)

18 But he [who had been given the electroweak interaction] that had received one [talent] went and dug in the earth, and hid [the Lambda] his lord's money.

19 After a long time, the lord of those servants [returned], and reckoned with them.

JUDAH (CALLED JUDAH) SOUGHT KNOWLEDGE

20 And so he that had received five talents came and brought another five talents, saying,

Innate Traits

Lord, you delivered five talents to me. Behold, beside them, I have gained five talents more. 21
His lord said unto him, Well done, thou good and faithful servant: thou hast been faithful over a
few things, I will make thee ruler over many things: enter thou into the joy of thy lord.

Israel Helper

22 He also that had received two talents came and said, Lord, thou delivered two talents to
me: one brings about new life, the other destroys compromised mass within life. Behold, I have
gained two other talents beside them. 23 His Lord said unto him, Well done, good and faithful
servant. You have been faithful over a few things, I will make you ruler over many things. You
enter into the joy of your Lord.

Jerusalem (called Jerusalem)

24 Then he [Jerusalem, of the river Hiddekel, where there are deceptions and hidden motivations], which had received the one talent [to teach hard lessons] came. And [he] said, Lord, I knew you. And [I know] that you are a hard man [a nucleus encased in an electron shell. [You] reap [quark-antiquark pairs as two of the eight gametes carried by gluon], where [and of which] you have not sown [your seed, protons, gluons and neutrons].

[You] gather [Ephesus and Sardis, the Gentiles from wombs] where you have not strawed.

25 And I was afraid and went and hid [knowledge of the electroweak interaction] your talent, in the earth [in particles, protons, gluons and neutrons]. Look there, you have what is yours.

26 His lord answered and said to him, You wicked and slothful servant. You knew that I reap where I did not sow, and gather where I have not strawed [placed my DNA].

27 You ought to have put my money [your knowledge] to the exchangers [who reward
knowledge with understanding, and understanding with wisdom]. And then at my coming I
should have received my own [talent] with usury [interest]. 28 Take therefore the talent from him
and give it to [Judah], he which has ten talents.

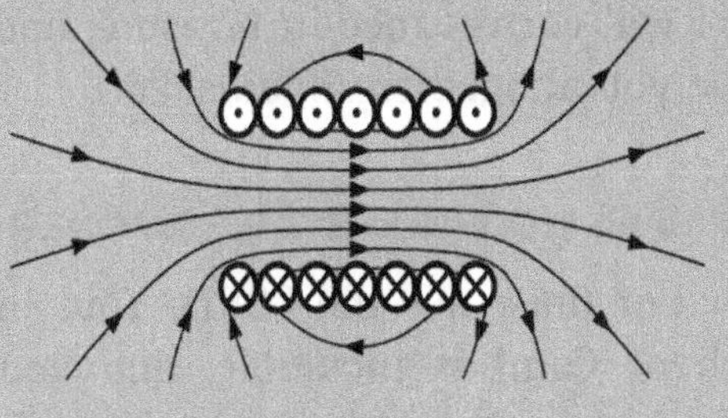

VFPt Solenoid
Magnetism, the spider, generating electricity.

29 For to every one that has [knowledge],
[understanding] shall be given. [It will grow] and he
shall have abundance. But from him that has not [little
understanding], [it] shall be taken away, even that which
he has. 30 And you cast the unprofitable servant into
outer darkness [the mind filled with empty space, without
light]. [Out there] shall be weeping [by magnetism] and
gnashing of teeth [by electricity].

Matthew 25:14-30 KJV

Restoration for the Jewels

1 The word that came to Jeremiah [Judah] from
the LORD, saying, 2 Thus speaks the LORD God
of Israel, saying, Write thee all the words that I
have spoken unto you in a book.

The Land Promised

3 For, lo, the days come, saith the LORD, that
I will bring again the captivity of my people
Israel and Judah, saith the LORD: and I will
cause them to return to the land[1] that I gave to
their fathers, and they shall possess it.

4 And these are the words that the LORD
spake concerning Israel and concerning Judah. 5
For thus saith the LORD; We have heard a voice
of trembling, of fear, and not of peace.

In league with photon

6 Ask you now, and see whether a man doth
travail with child? Wherefore do I see every man
with his hands on his loins [phallus], as a woman
in travail, and all faces are turned into paleness?

7 Alas! For that day is great, so that none is
like it: It is even the time of Jacob's trouble; but
he shall be saved out of it.

8 For it shall come to pass in that day, saith
the LORD of hosts [radon Higgs boson, energy,
mass and light], that I will break his yoke from
off your neck, and will burst your bonds, and
strangers [photon, Ephesus with Sardis] shall no
more serve themselves of him:

9 But they shall serve [Atom Lambda] the
LORD their God, and [gluon strong nuclear]
David their king, whom I will raise up unto them.

10 Therefore, fear you not, O my servant
Jacob, saith the LORD; neither be dismayed, O
Israel [the Jewels]: for, lo, I will save you from
afar [even from the sun], and [I will save] your
seed from [fecal matter and urine] the land of
their captivity [in the electromagnetic field];
And Jacob shall return, and shall be in rest, and
be quiet, and none shall make him afraid.

11 For I am with you, says the LORD, to save you:
though I make a full end of all nations whither
I have scattered you [with electromagnetic
scattering], yet will I not make a full end of thee:
but I will correct thee in measure, and will not
leave you altogether unpunished.

Israel wounded by her magnetism

12 For thus says the LORD, Your bruise [the
birth of Cain] is incurable, and your wound
[by the serpent] is grievous. 13 There is none to
plead your cause, that you may be bound up:

1 The land is mass and light, every energy pod, designed for the living in the gravitational field. This is the land promised. The corrupt bodies we wear today are imprisoned in the electromagnetic field.

"... And you shall be my people, and I will be your God."

You have no healing medicines. 14 All your
lovers have forgotten you; they seek you not;
for I have wounded you with the wound of an
enemy, with the chastisement of a cruel one,
for the multitude of thine iniquity; because
your sins were increased. 15 Why cry you for
your affliction? Your sorrow is incurable for the
multitude of thine iniquity: because your sins
were increased, I have done these things unto
you.

16 Therefore all they that devour you shall be devoured; and all your adversaries, every one of them, shall go into captivity; and they that spoil you shall be a spoil, and all that prey upon you will I give for a prey.

Restoration

17 For I will restore health unto you, and I will heal you of your wounds, says the LORD; because they called you an Outcast, saying, This is Zion, whom no man seeks after.

18 Thus saith the LORD; Behold, I will bring again the captivity of Jacob's tents [intentions], and have mercy on his dwelling places;

And [Jerusalem] the city shall be built upon her own heap [mass], and the palace [e'phod] shall remain after the manner thereof.

19 And out of them [Judah, Israel and Jerusalem] shall proceed thanksgiving and the voice of them that make merry: and I will multiply them, and they shall not be few; I will also glorify them, and they shall not be small.

20 Their children also shall be as aforetime, and their congregation shall be established before me, and I will punish all that oppress them.

21 And their Nobles [protons and neutrons] shall be of themselves, and their governor [gluon] shall proceed from the midst of them; and I will cause him to draw near, and he shall approach unto me: For who is this that engaged his heart to approach unto me? says the LORD.

22 And you [Judah, Israel and Jerusalem] shall be my people, and I [Atom Lambda] will be your God.

23 Behold, the whirlwind of the LORD goes forth with fury, a continuing whirlwind: it shall fall with pain upon the head of the wicked [Jewels and the Gentiles alike].

24 The fierce anger of the LORD shall not return, until he have done it, and until he have performed the intents of his heart: In the latter days you shall consider it. ✍

Jeremiah 30:1-24 KJV

Michelangelo, The First day of Creation
1510

Genesis 1. Atom Lambda (proton) surrounded by the four universal forces. Clockwise: strong Gravity wears the white headband; gluon strong nuclear with magnetism on his back; electromagnetism follows gluon strong nuclear; electroweak-weak, the black angel is posing to show off his beauty.

Revelation 1

Jesus Christ Lamb of God

Who is God?

The Lord God is Atom Lambda, the singularity. The beginning of all things visible.

The Father is strong Gravity.

The throne of God is the sun, whose hydrogen gives life to all living masses. And his throne is replicated in the hindbrain of the living.

We are lambdas; each person a singularity. Without Lambda in the hindbrain, we could not think, move, breathe or live.

This is the Revelation of Jesus Christ
[Atom Lambda], which [strong Gravity]
God gave to him, to show to his servants [the]
things which must shortly come to pass. And
he sent and signified it by his angel, [Gabriel,
the weak force] unto his servant John [the
Gentiles, converted]: 2 [John is he] who bare
record of [magnetism] the word of God, and
of the testimony of Jesus Christ, and of all
things that he saw.

3 Blessed is he that reads [interprets], and they that hear the words of this prophecy, and keep those things which are written therein*: for the time [of the end of the age of the Gentiles] is at hand.

Asia

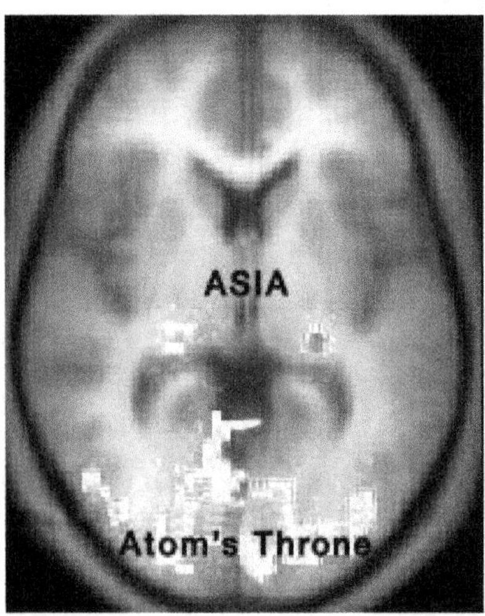

Asia refers to the east, the midbrain, where the sun also rises. The two lights at the midbrain are the two perspectives of gluon strong nuclear. Ourania, on the right is peaceful; Pandemos, on the left is where the dead or dying mass is destroyed.

4 John [writes] to the seven churches [minds and e'phods] which are in Asia.

Grace be to you, and peace from him which is [alive], and which was [dead], and which is to come [at the end of this age][1]; and from the seven Spirits [particles of universal light: bosons and gluons] which are before his throne.

5 And from Jesus Christ, who is the faithful
witness, and the first begotten of the dead, and
the prince of the kings of the earth. Unto him
that loved us, and washed us from our sins[2] in
his own blood [his deoxyribonucleic acid]. 6 And
[Jesus Christ] has made us kings [with crowns,
the crown of the head] and priests [those who
think, consider, make choices and pray] to God
[Atom Lambda] and his Father [strong Gravity].
To him [Jesus Christ] be glory and dominion for

1 By the law of conservation, whereas energy, mass and light cannot be destroyed. It changes form.

2 Sin means without, having no access to Atom Lambda and wisdom in the gravitational field. Sins are physical and mental maladies acquired when we left the presence of Atom Lambda, living as dead in the electromagnetic field, following the customs of the Gentiles, eating their food.

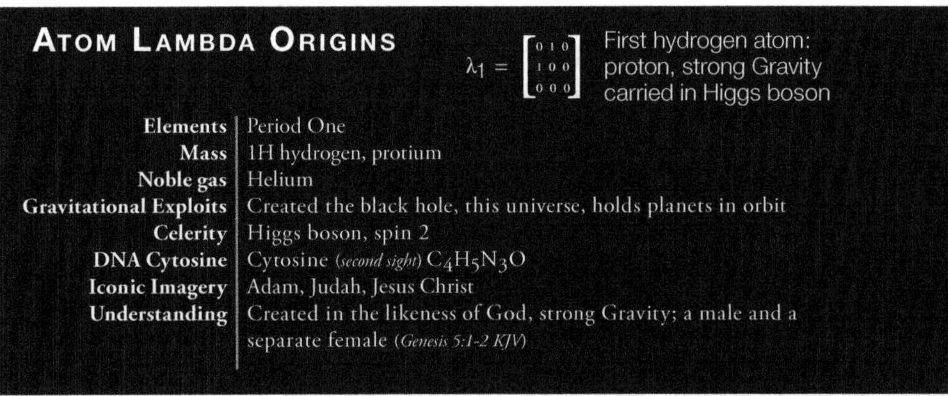

Atom Lambda Origins

$$\lambda_1 = \begin{bmatrix} 0 & 1 & 0 \\ 1 & 0 & 0 \\ 0 & 0 & 0 \end{bmatrix}$$

First hydrogen atom: proton, strong Gravity carried in Higgs boson

Elements	Period One
Mass	1H hydrogen, protium
Noble gas	Helium
Gravitational Exploits	Created the black hole, this universe, holds planets in orbit
Celerity	Higgs boson, spin 2
DNA Cytosine	Cytosine *(second sight)* $C_4H_5N_3O$
Iconic Imagery	Adam, Judah, Jesus Christ
Understanding	Created in the likeness of God, strong Gravity; a male and a separate female *(Genesis 5:1-2 KJV)*

"... From Jesus Christ, who is the faithful witness ..."

ever and ever. Amen.

7 Behold, he [Atom Lambda] comes with clouds [of the sky and the clouds that are the cerebrum and cerebellar cortex, the brain]. And every eye [the bosons, the gluons, the photons] shall see him; and they [of the electroweak-electromagnetism-weak interaction] also, which pierced him [with electricity]. And all kindreds of the earth [Jewels and Gentiles] shall wail [with magnetism] because of him. Even so, Amen.

8 I am Alpha and Omega, the beginning and the ending, says the Lord, which is [alive], and which was [dead], and which is to come [at the end of this age], the Almighty.

9 I, John [the Gentiles],

(Who also am your brother, and companion in tribulation, and in the kingdom and patience of Jesus Christ),

Was in the isle that is called Patmos [the hand] for [magnetism] the word of God [strong Gravity], and for the testimony of Jesus Christ.

10 I was in the Spirit [the Higgs boson, strong
Gravity's light, in the gravitational field] on the
Lord's day [period seven, the seventh day of
creation], and [I] heard behind me a great voice
[thunder], as of a trumpet, 11 Saying,

I am Alpha and Omega, the first and the last and, What you see write in a book, and send it unto the seven churches [minds, lights emanating from the hindbrain, with thoughts generated from the forebrain], which are in Asia [the midbrain]:

To Ephesus [the Gentiles, a reasoning mind in a female body];

And to Smyrna [Judah the scientist, the analytical mind in a male e'phod];

And to Pergamos [Israel the helper, the compassionate mind in a male e'phod];

And to Thyatira [Jerusalem, a Z boson (manic) or W^3 boson (reasoning) in a male or female e'phod;

And unto Sardis [the Gentiles, manic mind in a male body];

And unto Philadelphia [Judah the scientist, the analytical mind in a female e'phod];

And unto Laodicea [Israel the helper, the compassionate mind in a female e'phod; the avenger].

12 And I turned to see the voice that spake
with me. And being turned, I saw seven golden
candlesticks [e'phods lit synaptically from
head to toe]. 13 And in the midst of the seven

candlesticks [there was] one [Atom Lambda in the hindbrain] the like unto [Atom Lambda in the sun] the Son of man.

[Atom Lambda is] clothed with [Gravity], a garment [that covers from the top of the head] down to the foot. And [he is] girt about the paps [from the stomach, the pelvic to the thighs] with [gluon strong nuclear] a golden girdle.

14 His head [electricity] and his hairs [magnetism were] white like wool, as white as snow. And his eyes [the Higgs bosons] were as a flame of fire [the sun].

15 And his feet [electroweak or weak interaction were] like unto fine brass, as if they burned in a furnace.

And his voice as the sound of many [hydrogen] waters [the voice of every person].

16 And he had in his right hand seven [gluon] stars:

And out of his mouth went a sharp two-edged sword [Z or W^3 boson, a teacher, a disciplinarian]:

And his countenance was as the sun shines in his strength [with solar prominence erupting].

17 And when I saw him, I fell at his feet as dead. And he laid his right hand upon me, saying to me,

Fear not; I am the first and the last: 18 I am he
that lives, and was dead; and, behold, I am alive
for evermore*, Amen. And have the keys of hell
[magnetism] and of death [electricity].

19 Write the things which you have seen, and
the things which are, and the things which shall
be hereafter [at the end of this age]: 20 [Write
of] the mystery of the seven stars which you
saw in my right hand, and the seven golden
candlesticks. The seven stars are the angels of
the seven churches.

And the seven candlesticks [e'phods, bodies of people] which you saw are the seven churches [seven minds emanating from brains that sit atop e'phods, where all may think, consider, reason and choose]. ✍

Revelation 1:1-20 KJV

Delphi understands

Libyan builds, heals

These four sibyls, illustrated by Michelangelo, are four of the five sibyls, two of which are conjoined as one. Delphi carries the behaviour and properties of Strong Gravity. The Libyan sibyl is gluon strong nuclear. The Erythaean sibyl is the weak or electroweak force, designs, teaches and disciplines, fate and fortune for all. The Cumaen with Persian sibyl is the visible child of electromagnetism

Erythaean designs, teaches, disciplines

Cumaen with hidden Persian sibyl confusion

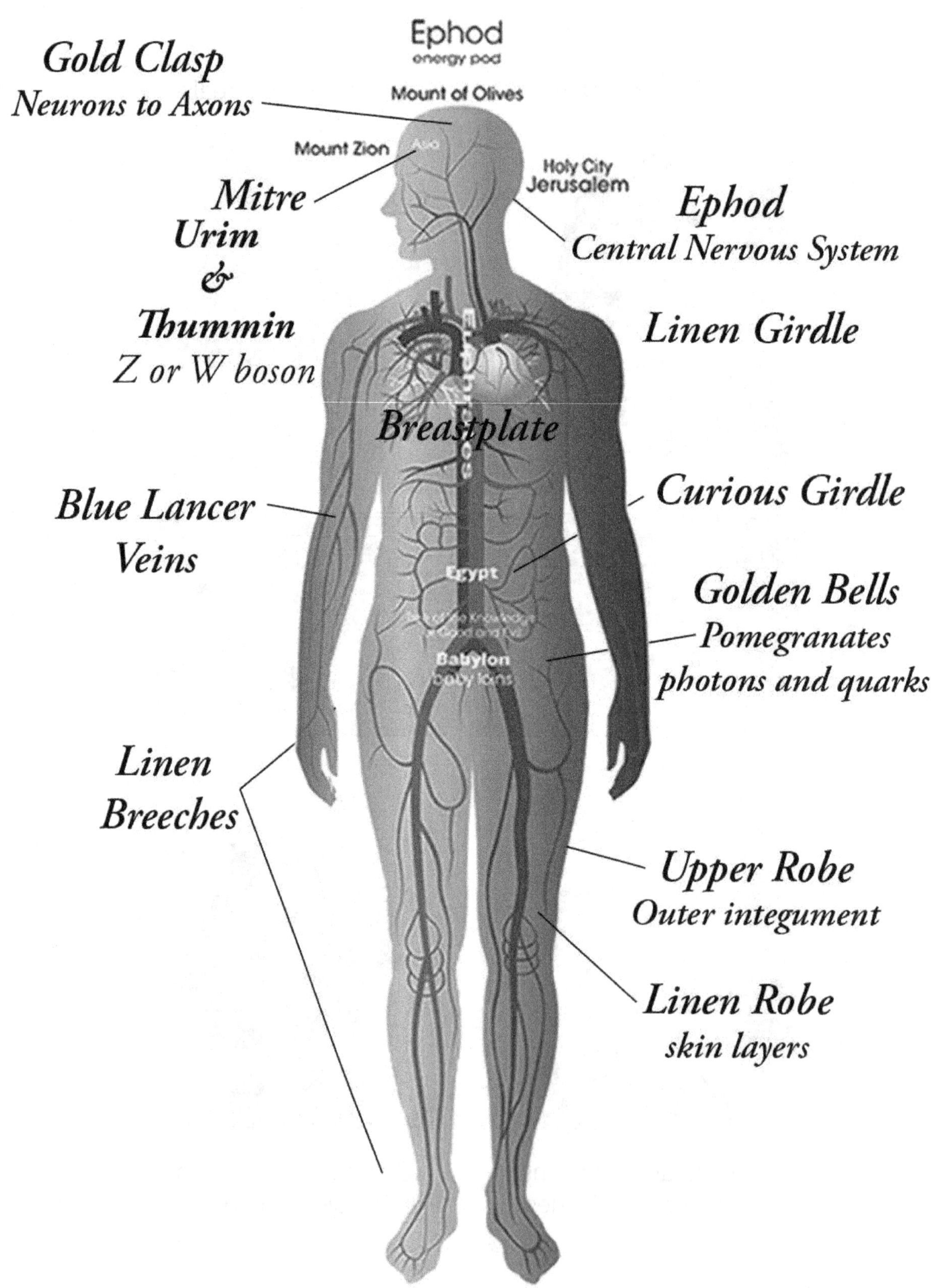
Ephod
energy pod
Gold Clasp
Neurons to Axons
Mount of Olives
Mount Zion
Holy City
Jerusalem
Mitre
Ephod
Central Nervous System
Urim
&
Thummin
Z or W boson
Linen Girdle
Breastplate
Curious Girdle
Blue Lancer
Veins
Egypt
Golden Bells
Pomegranates
photons and quarks
Babylon
Linen
Breeches
Upper Robe
Outer integument
Linen Robe
skin layers

Revelation 2

First Four Churches

Ephesus

Electricity, Cain (Sardis), is hidden in magnetism, Abel (Ephesus)
Electromagnetism
Electricity and poison are a dangerous combination together; but certain death if separate.

Exploits of Jesus Christ with Atom Lambda

1 Unto the [Z, photon with W boson merged as one], the angel of the church of Ephesus write:

Aurora Consurgens, Conjoined twins
15th century
Photon is the vulture speaking lies in their ears, tools to trap the innocent. Carrying a bat with a strong smell of urine, the female is magnetism. By electricity, the male carries a rabbit, smelling of fecal matter, his mind set on acts of reproduction. Their acts of destruction by touch, account for the many dead birds, mass, flesh.

These things says [Jesus Christ Atom Lambda], he that holds the seven [gluon] stars [mass and light] in his right hand. [Atom Lambda is he] who walks in the midst of the seven golden candlesticks [the e'phod (energy pod) lit by neurons, dendrites, axon terminals in an impressive a synaptic light show].

Innate Ways and Means

2 I know your [magnetic] works, and your labour, and your patience. And [I] how you cannot bear them [that are rooted in electricity], which are evil.

And you have [judged and] tried them which say they are apostles [who seek the truth], and [have found that they] are not [seeking truth]. And [you] have found them [to be] liars.

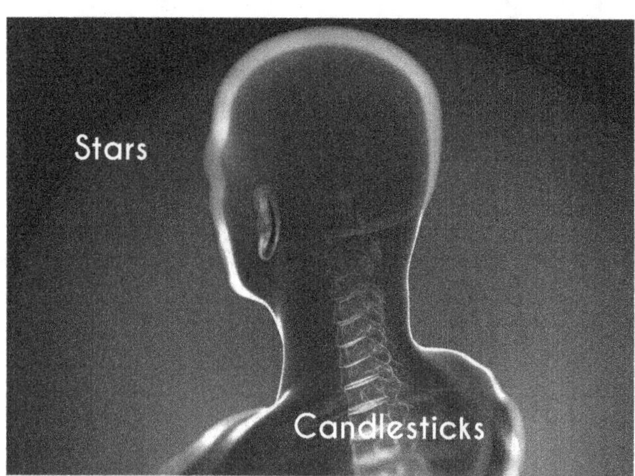

3 And [you, Ephesus] have borne [favor with God in charity]. And [you] have patience [like strong Gravity]. And for [Jesus Christ] my name's sake, [you] have laboured, and have not fainted.

Caution

4 Nevertheless, I have somewhat against you because you have left [strong Gravity, your coupling constant], your first love. 5 Remember

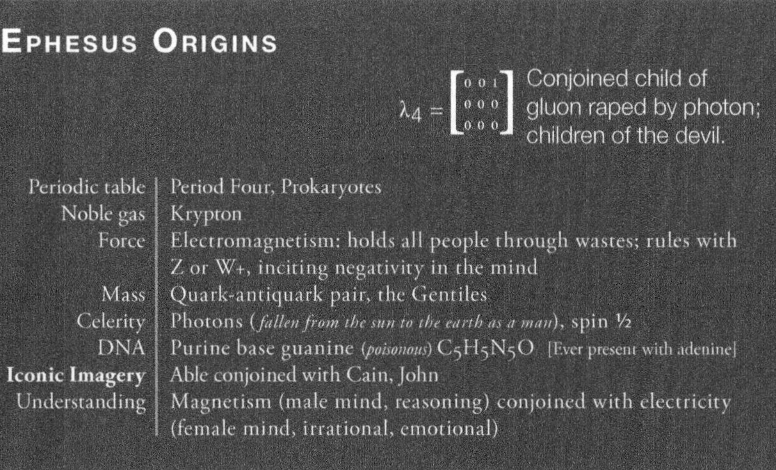

Ephesus Origins

$$\lambda_4 = \begin{bmatrix} 0 & 0 & 1 \\ 0 & 0 & 0 \\ 0 & 0 & 0 \end{bmatrix}$$ Conjoined child of gluon raped by photon; children of the devil.

Periodic table	Period Four, Prokaryotes
Noble gas	Krypton
Force	Electromagnetism: holds all people through wastes; rules with Z or W+, inciting negativity in the mind
Mass	Quark-antiquark pair, the Gentiles
Celerity	Photons (*fallen from the sun to the earth as a man*), spin ½
DNA	Purine base guanine (*poisonous*) $C_5H_5N_5O$ [Ever present with adenine]
Iconic Imagery	Able conjoined with Cain, John
Understanding	Magnetism (male mind, reasoning) conjoined with electricity (female mind, irrational, emotional)

therefore [the sun, the bladder of Atom Lambda], from where you are fallen, and repent, and do the first works, or else I will come to you quickly, and will remove your candlestick [e'phod] out of his place [out of DNA replication], except you repent.

6 But this you have, that you hate the deeds of the Nicolaitans [liars, with hidden motives, full of trickery], which I also hate.

To the Reader

7 He that has an ear, let him hear what [Atom Lambda] the Spirit says unto the churches; To him that overcomes [the temptations designed by the Z, photon and W3 merged as one] will I give to eat of [proton], the tree of life, which is in the midst of the paradise of God [Atom Lambda]. ✍

Revelation 2:1-7 KJV

Raphael, Mother and Child
1503
Image of photon electromagnetism and her son Cain, born from a quark-antiquark seed.

Smyrna

CYRUS
[sahy-ruh s]
A homograph: C-yr-us, -See You're Us: We are forces of energy, mass and light; the sun; humiliates liars in contests of truth versus deception.

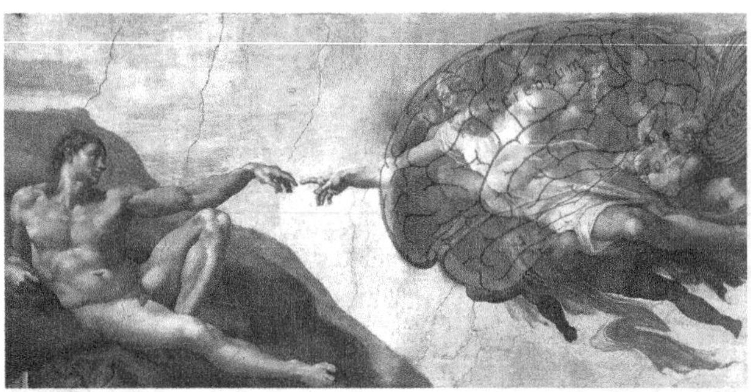

MICHELANGELO, CREATION OF ADAM
1508–1512
Adam touching Atom Lambda in the hindbrain, where he is surrounded by the mass and light particles in the nucleus of the atom.

EXPLOITS OF JESUS CHRIST WITH ATOM LAMBDA

8 And to the [Higgs boson] angel of the church in Smyrna write:

These things says the first [the singularity, the beginning of all things visible]; and the last [the radon higgs boson in Atom Lambda in the hindbrain]; which was dead [crucified with Jesus Christ]; and [by the law of conservation] is alive [a spirit, the Higgs boson, which rose up and was collected in the light of the sun].

INNATE WAYS AND MEANS

9 I know your [gravitational] works [slow and methodical, steady]; and tribulation [accused falsely of many vile things], and poverty*

AURORA CONSURGENS, THE CHASTE ANGEL
15th Century
Higgs boson, the chaste angel. Her feet are webbed like the feet of a bird. Suffering interference by electromagnetism, she stumbles and sometimes fall.

[existing from meal to meal].

(But you are rich)! [Judah is rich in knowledge, understanding and wisdom which brings him blessing and unexpected financial gains.]

CAUTION

10 Fear none of those things which you shall suffer. Behold, the devil [Z or W^3 boson, led by photon] shall cast some of you into prison, [so]

that you may be tried.

And you shall have <u>tribulation</u> [be tested for <u>ten days</u> [every day of your life].

Reward

Be faithful unto death, and I will give you a crown of life.

To the Reader

11 He that hath an ear, let him hear what the Spirit saith unto the churches; He that overcomes shall not be hurt of the second death.[3] ✍

Revelation 2:8-11 KJV

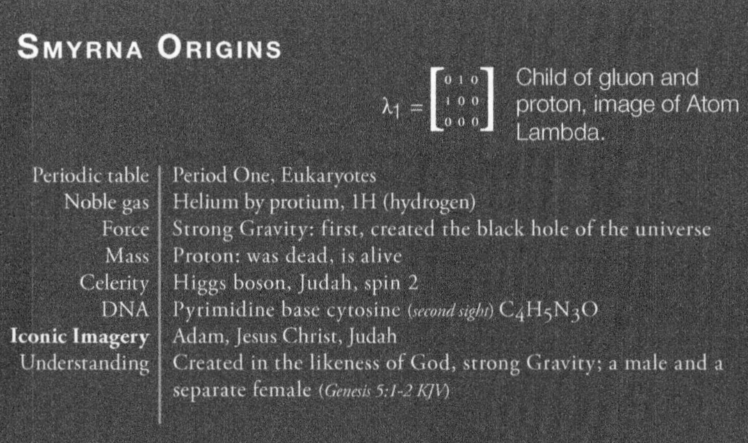

Smyrna Origins

$$\lambda_1 = \begin{bmatrix} 0 & 1 & 0 \\ 1 & 0 & 0 \\ 0 & 0 & 0 \end{bmatrix}$$ Child of gluon and proton, image of Atom Lambda.

Periodic table	Period One, Eukaryotes
Noble gas	Helium by protium, 1H (hydrogen)
Force	Strong Gravity: first, created the black hole of the universe
Mass	Proton: was dead, is alive
Celerity	Higgs boson, Judah, spin 2
DNA	Pyrimidine base cytosine *(second sight)* $C_4H_5N_3O$
Iconic Imagery	Adam, Jesus Christ, Judah
Understanding	Created in the likeness of God, strong Gravity; a male and a separate female *(Genesis 5:1-2 KJV)*

Michelangelo, Jesus Christ
1508-1512

By the light of the Higgs boson, Atom Lambda in the hindbrain, Jesus Christ is drawn into the sun. He is risen.

3 The first death is death of the body. The second death is destruction of the soul, the light, wherein the connection to Atom Lambda is severed.

Pergamos

Israel
[ĭz'rēəl]
A homograph: Is real. Gluon is a real light that rose up from the meconium passed of the Higgs boson, born of hydrogen. Meconium is cells, mucus and bile, stored in the intestines while in utero. By this, gluon is self lit and exceedingly strong.

Aurora Consurgens, Two sides of gluon strong nuclear
15th Century
Like all of Israel, gluon strong nuclear, Ourania, has a head and heart of gold. His alter ego, Pandemos, is as an aggressive female, a bird of prey, predatory, luring and destroying the weak.

Exploits of Jesus Christ with Atom Lambda

12 And to [gluon strong nuclear] the angel of the church in Pergamos write;

These things says he which has the sharp sword with two edges: [gluon strong nuclear is the sword.

She has two sides, Ourania for peace and Pandemos for war. Pergamos is Israel, "is real"];

Innate Ways and Means

13 I know your works [as helper, feeding the poor, tending the sick, defending the weak, as archangel Micheal], And [I know] where you dwell [in the midbrain, whose feet stand on the two lights on the Mount of Olives].

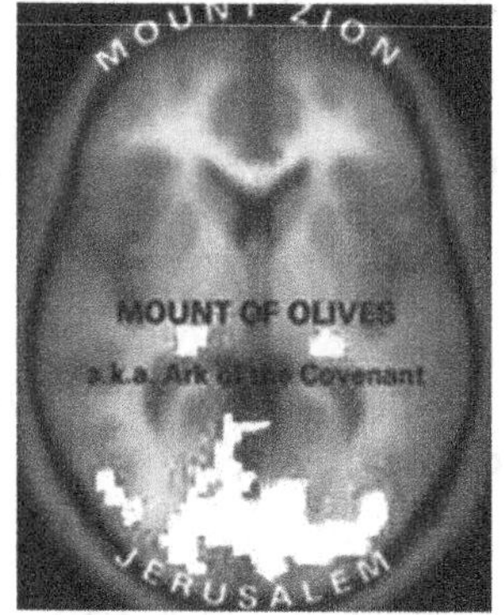

And [you reside in the reproductive system, spinning particles of mass into gametes: proton as Judah; gluon as Israel; neutron as Jerusalem the teacher, fate and fortune; quark as Sardis conjoined with an antiquark as Ephesus, your children],

[The reproductive system is] even where Satan's seat is [located: as magnetism (Satan) sits on the reproductive organs, drawing down wastes, fertilizer as fecal matter and watering the garden with urine].

And you hold fast [to] my name [Atom Lambda], and [you] have not denied my [faithfulness], Even in those days, wherein* Antipas [Ephesus, an antiquark] was my faithful martyr, who was slain among you, [in the electromagnetic field] where Satan [magnetism] dwells.

PERGAMOS ORIGINS

$\lambda_2 = \begin{bmatrix} 0 & -i & 0 \\ i & 0 & 0 \\ 0 & 0 & 0 \end{bmatrix}$ Third child of gluon and proton, image of Atom Lambda.

Periodic table	Period Two, Eukaryotes
Noble gas	Neon with Argon, Deuterium 2H (hydrogen)
Force	Strong Nuclear: a sharp sword with two edges
Mass	Gluon: Ourania or Pandemos, Israel
Celerity	Gluon: Ourania or Pandemos, Israel, spin 1
DNA	Pyrimidine base thymine *(thy will is my will)* $C_5H_6N_2O_2$
Iconic Imagery	Eve mother of all; Jacob genetic octet; David ruler of all
Understanding	Created in the likeness of God; a male and a separate female *(Genesis 5:1-2 KJV)*

CAUTION

14 But I have a few things against you: because you [gluon] have there [within you] them [the quark antiquark pairs] that hold the doctrine of Balaam [the Z or W3 boson], who taught* Balac [photon electromagnetism how] to cast a stumblingblock before [Judah, Israel and Jerusalem], the children of Israel.

Balaam [taught Adam and Eve] to eat things [fecal matter and urine] sacrificed unto idols [quark-antiquark pairs, photons]. And [Balaam taught them] to commit fornication [to leave the safety of Atom Lambda and the gravitational field, to join their bodies and minds to photon electromagnetism, and die moaning with the taste of excrement in their mouths].

AURORA CONSURGENS, QUARK-ANTIQUARK PAIR CONSUMING WASTE *15th Century*

Like pigs, quarks consume their own fecal matter, powering electricity; antiquarks drink the urine and menstrual blood contaminated with living death.

15 So have you also [embraced] them that hold the doctrine [that is rooted in deception] of the Nicolaitans. [They keep alive the deceptions embedded in and surrounding every important religious event: they worship photon as St. Nick; and celebrate him at Christmas in stories, poems, songs]. [Of] which [deception is a] thing [that] I [Atom Lambda] hate.

16 Repent; or else I will come unto thee quickly, and will fight against them with the sword of my mouth.

FOR THE READER

17 He that has an ear, let him hear what the Spirit says to the churches.

REWARDS

To him that overcomes I will give to eat of the hidden manna [from strong Gravity, wisdom], And will give him a white stone [Atom Lambda, the sun], and in the stone a new name [will be] written,

Which no man knows saving he that receives it. ✍

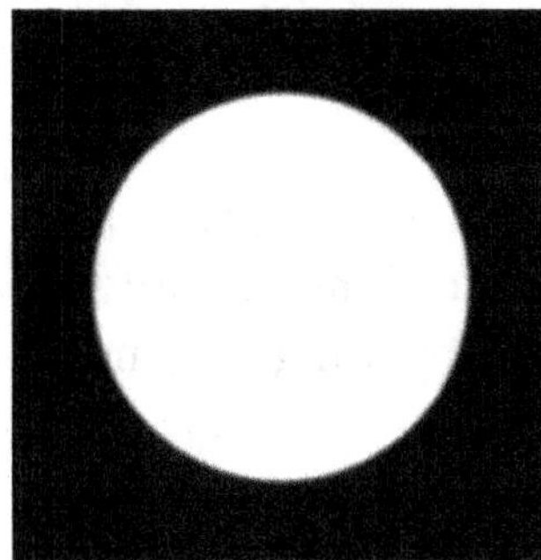

SUN, ALPHA: THE WHITE STONE

Revelation 2:12-17 KJV

Thyatira

Jerusalem
[ji-roo-suh-luh m, -zuh-]
A homograph; name for the Z or W boson, the disciplinarian, teacher: He rules all men - people. With throne in the forebrain, he directs the eyes toward evil to test all people.

Aurora Consurgens, The Black Angel on Black Ball
15th Century

The Black angel is the W^3 boson, born of the Z boson in the electromagnetic field. Rescued and cared for in the gravitational field by Atom Lambda. For mankind, she is fate or fortune; testing and rewarding or disciplining.

Exploits of Jesus Christ with Atom Lambda

18 And unto [Z or W^3 boson] the angel of the church in Thyatira write;

These things saith the Son of God, who hath his eyes [bosons] like unto a flame of fire [the electroweak interaction, expressing his nerve through electricity],

And his feet are like fine brass [the weak interaction, three modes of magnetism];

Innate Ways and Means for the Z boson

19 I know your works, [for as Abram, the Z boson was given to test the king using his wife as bait and reaped great rewards];

And charity, [giving to people and animals];

And service, [to your fellowman in the hour of need];

And faith, [to Atom Lambda, following his commands];

And your patience, [while you wait for deliverance from confusion];

And your works [teaching the masses, like Paul, showing appreciation to the ones who learn and praising Atom Lambda for the gifts that make you great in the eyes of Atom Lambda];

And [Atom Lambda has found] the last [works of the W^3 boson] to be more [beneficial, effective] than the first [of the Z boson, who wins by yelling, screaming and attacking physically, beating, like electricity, the Hittite].

Caution

20 Notwithstanding, I [Jesus Christ Atom Lambda] have a few things against you [Z boson, electroweak force, creator of photon].

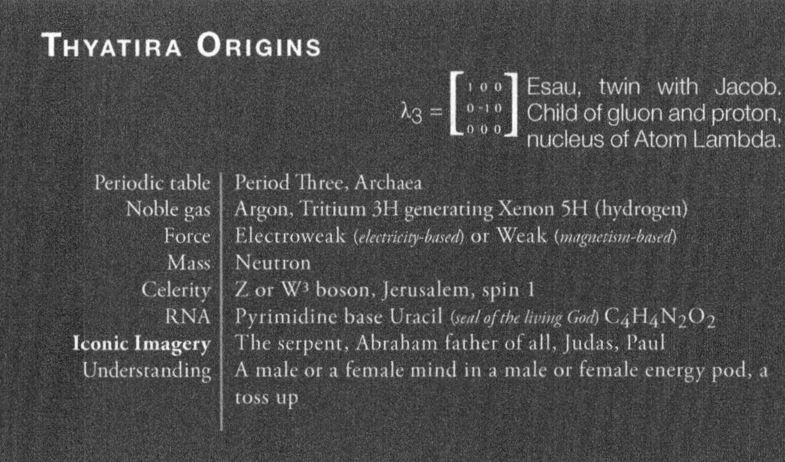

Thyatira Origins

$\lambda_3 = \begin{bmatrix} 1 & 0 & 0 \\ 0 & -1 & 0 \\ 0 & 0 & 0 \end{bmatrix}$ Esau, twin with Jacob. Child of gluon and proton, nucleus of Atom Lambda.

Periodic table	Period Three, Archaea
Noble gas	Argon, Tritium 3H generating Xenon 5H (hydrogen)
Force	Electroweak *(electricity-based)* or Weak *(magnetism-based)*
Mass	Neutron
Celerity	Z or W^3 boson, Jerusalem, spin 1
RNA	Pyrimidine base Uracil *(seal of the living God)* $C_4H_4N_2O_2$
Iconic Imagery	The serpent, Abraham father of all, Judas, Paul
Understanding	A male or a female mind in a male or female energy pod, a toss up

Because you suffer [allow] that woman Jezebel [photon electromagnetism], which calls herself a prophetess, to teach [lies tempered with truth] and to seduce my servants [arousing their loins while displaying lewd pictures in their minds] to commit fornication [joining their bodies and souls to photon, enabling the devil with Satan to steal the children of Atom Lambda];

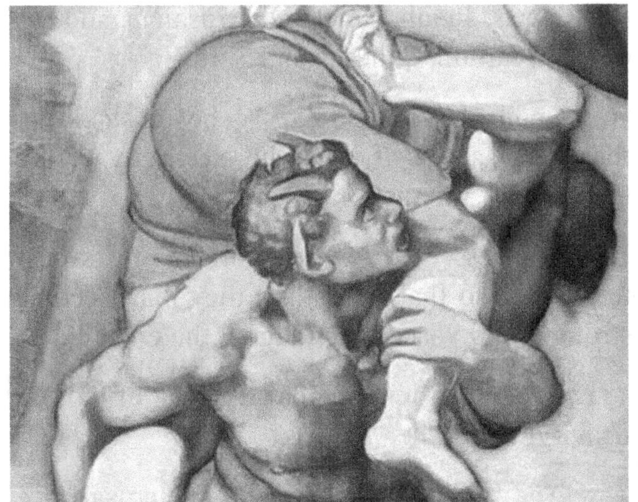

Michelangelo, Abduction of Persephone
15th Century
Israel (Eve) is abducted from the gravitational field by photon electromagnetism, who has two horns like the lambda, but speaks with the voice of a dragon.

And to eat things, [fecal matter, urine and menstrual blood] sacrificed to idols: [photons, quark-antiquark pairs or Z bosons].

21 And I gave her space [time] to repent of her
fornication; and she repented not. 22 Behold, I
will cast her into a [perpetual death] bed,

And those that commit adultery with her [will be cast] into great tribulation [mental anguish, physical unrest as the forces of life shall be taken away, except mag, financial, social], except they repent of their deeds.

23 And I will kill her children [the Gentiles, Sardis and Ephesus] with death [electricity];

And all the churches[1] shall know that I [Jesus Christ Atom Lambda] am he [in the hindbrain] which searches the reins [by the forces (horses) that reside within the living to see where they are being led]. And [I search the] hearts[2] [to see that which is treasured]. And I [Atom Lambda] will give unto every one of you [Z or W3] according to your works.

Innate Ways and Means for the W^3 Boson

24 But unto you [Jerusalem W^3 boson or Z] I say,

1 Churches are energy pods with minds that contemplate, voices that speak and arms that perform work and legs and feet that walk

2 For where your treasure is, there will your heart be also. Matthew 6:21 KJV

Charity
['tʃœɹɪti]
Born with the inclination to aid the poor, ill, or helpless, Jerusalem has innate benevolent tendencies, especially toward those in need or in disfavor.

As master of fate and fortune, he may demonstrate leniency in judging others.

Thorvaldsen, Ganymede offering water to Zeus.
Ganymede is the Z or W boson. Zeus is Atom Lambda, in the form of an eagle.

Neo-Hittite Chimera [Nicolaitans]
The lion is the W^3 boson, the leader. The goat, the head in helmet is the Z boson. The tail with the serpent head is photon, deceiver, destroyer.

And unto the rest [in Jerusalem, of SU(3), which includes photon electromagnetism] in Thyatira, as many as have not this doctrine, and which have not known the depths [evil declination] of Satan [magnetism], as they speak [to the masses, people]; I will put upon you no other burden.

25 But that which you have already hold fast till I come* [at the end of the age of the Gentiles].

Rewards for Jerusalem

26 And he that overcomes, and keeps my works unto the end, to him will I give power [to teach and reinforce precepts] over the nations [the Jewels, Judah, Israel and Jerusalem, and the Gentiles nation, Ephesus and Sardis]:

27 And he [Jerusalem Z or W^3 boson shall rule them with a rod of iron [the electricity of the electroweak interaction];

As the vessels of a potter shall they be broken to shivers [so that in healing they may become stronger and wiser, when facing the enemy]:

Even as I [Atom Lambda] received of [strong Gravity] my Father.[3]

28 And I will give him [Thyatira, Jerusalem Z or W^3 boson] the morning star [the sun, so full of promise and wisdom].

To the Reader

29 He that has an ear, let him hear what the Spirit says to the churches. ✍

Revelation 2:18-29 KJV

3 The Ram and the Goat, Daniel 8:1-27 KJV

Michelangelo, Last Judgment detail

1508-1512

The weak interaction, W boson, offers feces and urea concealed in the *membrum virile*, the male reproductive organ. The member is alive by the electricity in the blood; but will soon be dead in Peniel. In the left hand of the weak force is the electroweak interaction, shed as dead. The electroweak-weak interaction is an either-or force, either weak and logical or electroweak and raging like a tempest, Abram, Z boson or Ham, W boson, full of magnetism.

Three Crowns over three temples
A queen, an innocent, a thinker

Revelation 3

Last Three Churches

Sardis

Electricity, Cain (Sardis), is hidden in magnetism, Abel (Ephesus)
Electromagnetism
Electricity and poison are a dangerous combination together; but certain death if separate.

Flemish tapestry (Fates)
Circa 1510-1520)

As the Angel of the church in Sardis the Z boson is first. From Z came photon magnetism. The W boson is dressed in finery. Below on the ground is photon carrying electricity, dead as electricity dies of itself. Photon magnetism's foot rests on electricity.

1 And to [Z, photon with W boson merged in one light, of SU(3), the special unitary group] of the electroweak interaction]: the angel of the church in Sardis write:

Aurora Consurgens
15th century

Photon is the vulture speaking lies in their ears, tools to trap the innocent. Carrying a bat with a strong smell of urine, the female is magnetism. By electricity, the male carries a rabbit, set on acts of reproduction, rape, pedophilia. Their acts of destruction by touch, account for the many dead birds, magnetism throughout mass, flesh.

Exploits of Jesus Christ with Atom Lambda

These things says he [Atom Lambda] that

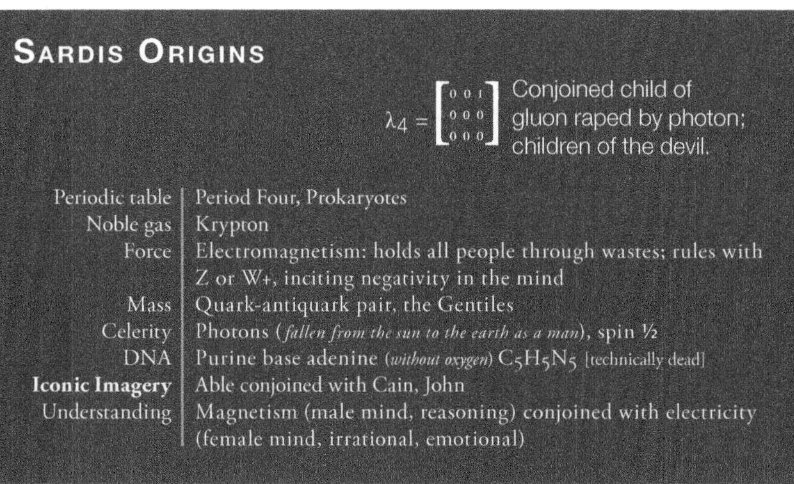

Sardis Origins

$$\lambda_4 = \begin{bmatrix} 0 & 0 & 1 \\ 0 & 0 & 0 \\ 0 & 0 & 0 \end{bmatrix}$$ Conjoined child of gluon raped by photon; children of the devil.

Periodic table	Period Four, Prokaryotes
Noble gas	Krypton
Force	Electromagnetism: holds all people through wastes; rules with Z or W+, inciting negativity in the mind
Mass	Quark-antiquark pair, the Gentiles
Celerity	Photons (*fallen from the sun to the earth as a man*), spin ½
DNA	Purine base adenine (*without oxygen*) $C_5H_5N_5$ [technically dead]
Iconic Imagery	Able conjoined with Cain, John
Understanding	Magnetism (male mind, reasoning) conjoined with electricity (female mind, irrational, emotional)

has the <u>seven Spirits of God</u> [lambdas, atoms, gametes that became zygotes, then embryos delivered as new born babes; each a unique individual, a singularity, a king with royal blood, by the father, Atom Lambda]; [Hallowed be your name.]

And [Atom Lambda has] the <u>seven stars</u> [1] [of the octet of stars born of gluon strong nuclear, the seven churches with eight lights, one hidden];

Michelangelo, Rebellious and Dying Slave
1513

The rebellious slave is Sardis, electricity, the walking dead, who follows the behaviour of the electroweak force with electromagnetism. The rebellious slave leans against the membrum virile, which rises by magnetism and dies by electricity, of itself. The dying slave is Ephesus, the empathetic, leaning against the shape of a vagina.

1 The seven stars light the way in the minds of the seven churches, directing the eye on Atom Lambda's command.

Michelangelo, Moses
1513–1515

Moses the Gentiles has two horns, voices, forces, electricity and magnetism. Moses was useful for extracting the Jewels from the electromagnetic field.

Innate Ways for Sardis

[You children of photon, generating electricity], I know your <u>works</u>: as a bully from childhood, destroyer of self-esteem, rape, pedophilia, murder, extortioner, and worse;

[I know] that you have a [genetic] <u>name</u> that [says] <u>you live</u>, and [because of the missing oxygen in your genetic code ($C_5H_5N_5$), you are [technically] <u>dead</u>, [the living dead from ancient tales].

Hope for the Gentiles

For we three Jewels are Atom Lambda's workmanship, placed in the nucleus of atoms to do the good works that strong Gravity, God, ordained before the world was made. So we should walk in, live by his scientific laws. Wherefore, remember that you Gentiles, quarks are flesh, the Uncircumcision, emitting electricity without reason. The antiquarks, mass, are the Circumcision, exuding magnetism. From the time of Cain, you Gentiles are aliens, electricity, in sin, without crystallization, without Atom Lambda. But then, from the bowels of gluon, the commonwealth of Israel, Eve, also came the strangers, Abel, magnetism. From the covenants of promise, they have no hope; alone in the world without Atom Lambda. But now in Jesus, you, who sometimes were far off in the electromagnetic field, are made closer by the purifying properties of DNA, the blood of Christ.

Ephesians 2:8-13 KJV

Caution

2 Be watchful, and strengthen [magnetism] the things which remain, [electricity] that are ready to die. For I have not found your works perfect before God.

3 Remember therefore *how* you have received [the truth of your existence] and heard [the voice of Atom Lambda],

And hold fast [to him], and repent.

If therefore you shall not watch, I will come on you as a thief [And snatch your DNA code from Jacob's ladder], And you shall not know what hour I will come upon you.

Rewards

4 You have a few names even in Sardis which have not defiled their garments [e'phods, minds];

And they shall walk with me in white [light, the sun]: for they are worthy.

5 He that overcomes, the same shall be clothed in white raiment [the light of the sun];

And I will not blot out his name out of the [genetic] book of life [DNA], but I will confess his name before my Father [strong Gravity], and before his angels [bosons, the six noble gases

Unknown, John the Apostle

from the six periods of the periodic table of the elements].

To the Reader

6 He that has an ear, let him hear what [Atom Lambda] the Spirit says to the churches. ✍

Revelation 3:1-6 KJV

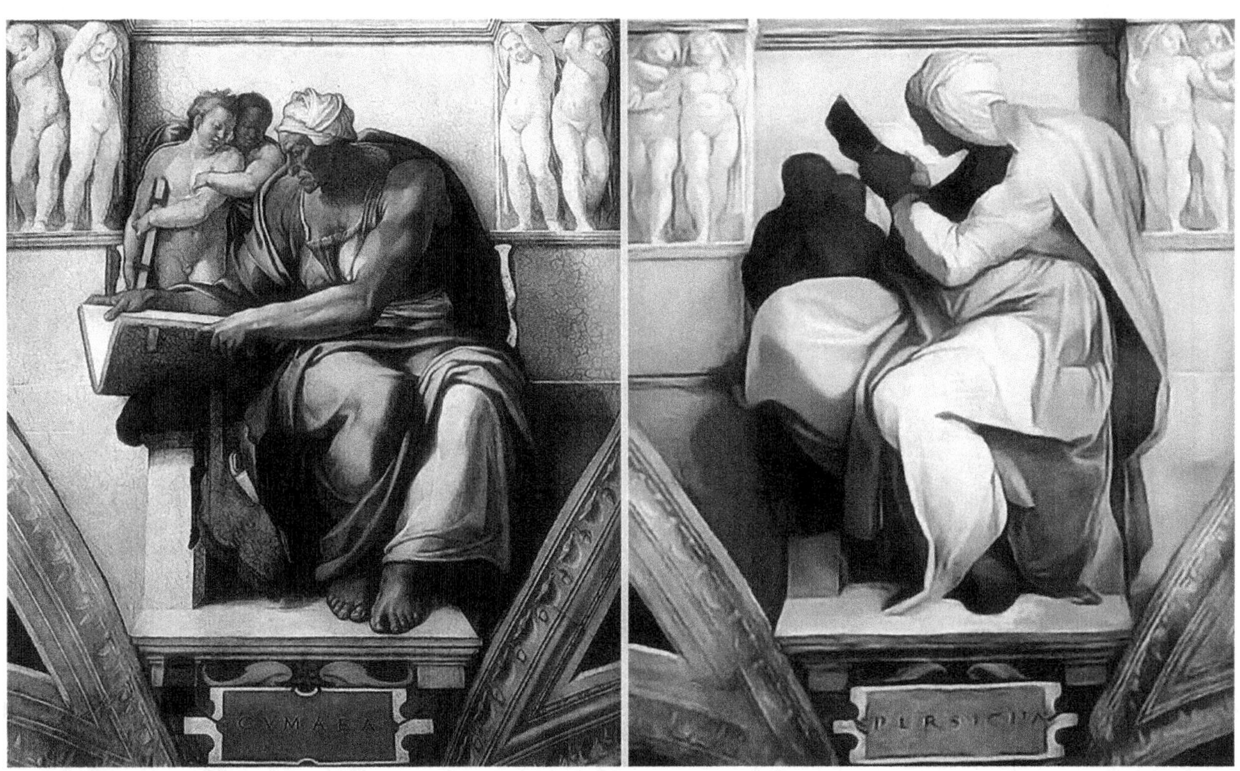

MICHELANGELO, THE SIBYLS
1510 and 1511

The Cumaen sibyl whose face you see is the force of magnetism, the learned one. Over her head is W^3 holding a large book. Clutching him is electricity, the Canaanite, before Cain was conceived. The face of the Persian sibyl is hidden. In the shadows are her intentions, a quark-antiquark pair. She is electricity, and electricity has no discernible face.

Philadelphia

Cyrus
[saby-ruh s]
A homograph: C-yr-us, -See You're Us: We are forces of energy, mass and light; the sun; humiliates liars in contests of truth versus deception.

Aurora Consurgens, The Chaste Angel
15th Century
The angel is the Higgs boson.

7 And to [the Higgs boson], the angel of the church in Philadelphia write;

Exploits of Jesus Christ, Atom Lambda

These things says [Atom Lambda], he that is holy [his actions justified],

He that is true [scientifically proven by physics and its laws, with genetic, anatomical and astrological proof],

He that has the key of David, [1]

Atom Lambda with three Jewels:
2008
Judah (proton), Israel(gluon) and Jerusalem (neutron).

He that opens [doors, creates opportunities], and no man shuts; And shuts [doors that should not be opened], and no man opens;

Innate Ways and Means

8 [Judah, Adam], I know your [scientific]

1 David is gluon strong nuclear, Israel. Gluon resides within proton. And though gluon is self-lit with his own brand of knowledge and understanding, he takes his wisdom from Atom Lambda, his gravitas from strong Gravity, and strong Gravity is God.

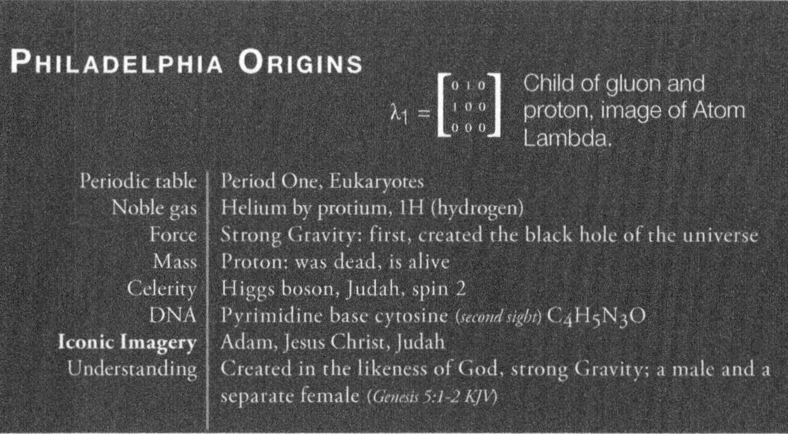

PHILADELPHIA ORIGINS

$\lambda_1 = \begin{bmatrix} 0 & 1 & 0 \\ 1 & 0 & 0 \\ 0 & 0 & 0 \end{bmatrix}$ Child of gluon and proton, image of Atom Lambda.

Periodic table	Period One, Eukaryotes
Noble gas	Helium by protium, 1H (hydrogen)
Force	Strong Gravity: first, created the black hole of the universe
Mass	Proton: was dead, is alive
Celerity	Higgs boson, Judah, spin 2
DNA	Pyrimidine base cytosine *(second sight)* $C_4H_5N_3O$
Iconic Imagery	Adam, Jesus Christ, Judah
Understanding	Created in the likeness of God, strong Gravity; a male and a separate female *(Genesis 5:1-2 KJV)*

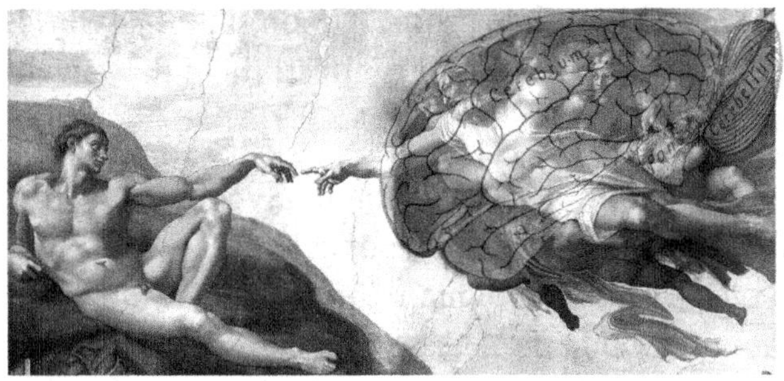

MICHELANGELO, CREATION OF ADAM
1508-1512
Adam touches the hand of Atom Lambda, who with the particles of mass, light and forces, resides in the hindbrain.

works:[2]

Behold, I have set before you an open door [knowledge, understanding and wisdom], and no man can shut it:

For [as strong Gravity in the earth is the weakest of all forces], you have a little strength, And have kept my word [laws, precepts], And have not denied my name [Atom Lambda].

9 Behold, I will make them [the Gentiles] of the synagogue [minds, like churches] of Satan [photon magnetism], which say they are Jews [because they appear in e'phods], and are not [Jewels], but [in the way of magnetism, they] do lie;

MICHELANGELO, LAST JUDGMENT
1508-1512
Judah the woman who fought the dragon and Jesus Christ.

Behold, I will make them [the Gentiles] to come and worship before your feet, and to know that I [Atom Lambda] have loved you.

10 Because you have kept the word of my patience [like Job; as gravity on earth is slow and patient], I also will keep you from the hour

2 The LORD God formed every beast of the gravitational field, and every fowl of the air; and brought them unto Adam to see what he would call them. Genesis 2:19-20 KJV

"... Behold, I have set before thee an open door ..."

of temptation [when photon electromagnetism arouses with pictures, thoughts, illusions and

Blake, Faith of Job Celebrated by bosons, angels
1793

Job is celebrated for his patience by the angels. When the morning Stars sang together, and all the sons of God shouted for joy... Job 38:7

mucus excreting from the sinus cavity in pelvic area]; which shall come* upon all the world [upon every person], to try [test] them that dwell upon the earth.

11 Behold, I [Atom Lambda] come quickly.
Hold that [your perseverance] fast, which you have, [so] that no man [lures you away from Atom Lambda and] takes your crown.

Rewards

12 He that overcomes I will make a pillar [of
light] in the temple [the Higgs boson] of [Atom Lambda] my God, and he shall go out [of the gravitational field, life, into the electromagnetic field, death] no more:

And I will write upon him the name of my God, and the name of the city of my God, which is new Jerusalem, which comes down out of heaven from my God:

And I will write upon him my new name.

For the reader

13 He that has an ear, let him hear what [Atom
Lambda] the [Holy] Spirit says to the churches [the minds of all people]. ✍

Revelation 3:7-13 KJV

Michelangelo, Sibyl at Delphi, Phila*delphi*a

The Delphic Sibyl reads the scroll, the small scroll of the Revelation. Behind her head is gluon and Z or W boson. Delphica is Higgs boson with gluon and the Z or W boson.

ISRAEL
[ĭz′rēəl]
A homograph: Is real. Gluon is a real light that rose up from the meconium passed of the Higgs boson, born of hydrogen. Meconium is cells, mucus and bile, stored in the intestines while in utero. By this, gluon is self lit and exceedingly strong.

Laodicea

"We dwell in him, and he in us."

14 And to the angel of the church of the Laodiceans write;

AURORA, MICHAEL, PROTECTOR AND MOTHER
The protector sitting on the lion is gluon, ruler of Atom Lambda's immunological armies. The female sitting on the lion with the beak and feet of a chicken is Eve or Jacob, mother of all.

EXPLOITS OF JESUS CHRIST, ATOM LAMBDA

These things says the Amen, [a-men is a homograph signifying "all men," as Atom Lambda is the principle component within all men, all atoms, forces, mass and light.]

[Like gluon strong nuclear, Atom Lambda is] the faithful and true witness [to life, observing all things, continually], [1]

[Hydrogen waters and mass is] the beginning of the creation of God;

INNATE WAYS AND MEANS

15 I know your works, that you are neither cold [scavenging in the electromagnetic field for food, pleasure];

Nor hot [wholly following truth in the gravitational field]:

I would [prefer that] you were cold or hot. 16
So then, because you are lukewarm, and neither cold nor hot, I will spue you out of my mouth.

17 Because you say*, I am rich [with a head of gold], and increased with goods [chest of immunological silver], and have need of nothing;

And [you do] not know that you are wretched, and miserable, and poor, and blind, and naked [vulnerable without Atom Lambda]:

18 I counsel you to buy gold [neurons, understanding] of me, tried in the fire, [so] that you may be rich [in knowledge, understanding and wisdom];

1 Hereby know we that we dwell in him, and he in us, because he hath given us of his Spirit [light]. 1 John 4:13 KJV

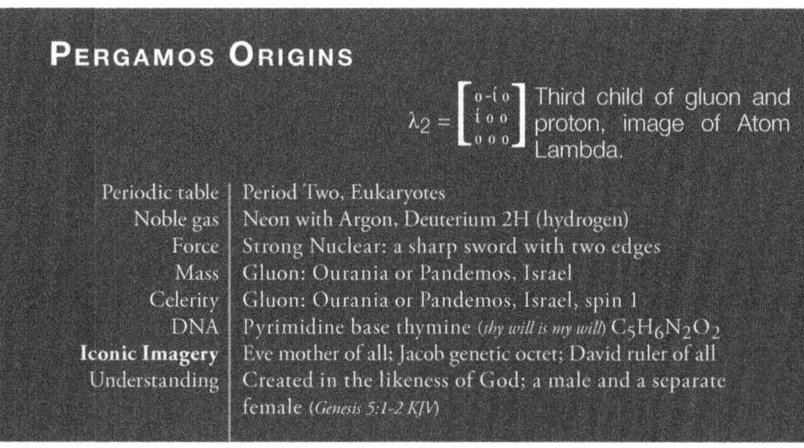

Pergamos Origins

$\lambda_2 = \begin{bmatrix} 0 & -i & 0 \\ i & 0 & 0 \\ 0 & 0 & 0 \end{bmatrix}$ Third child of gluon and proton, image of Atom Lambda.

Periodic table	Period Two, Eukaryotes
Noble gas	Neon with Argon, Deuterium 2H (hydrogen)
Force	Strong Nuclear: a sharp sword with two edges
Mass	Gluon: Ourania or Pandemos, Israel
Celerity	Gluon: Ourania or Pandemos, Israel, spin 1
DNA	Pyrimidine base thymine *(thy will is my will)* $C_5H_6N_2O_2$
Iconic Imagery	Eve mother of all; Jacob genetic octet; David ruler of all
Understanding	Created in the likeness of God; a male and a separate female *(Genesis 5:1-2 KJV)*

"As many as I love, I rebuke and chasten."

Wilhelm Rottermondt, Archangel Michael
Bonn, Gold plated lead. Michael (gluon strong nuclear) is the great red dragon.

And [buy] <u>white raiment</u> [light from the sun], [so] that you may be <u>clothed</u> [in truth], and [so] that the <u>shame of your nakedness</u> [magnetism] does not <u>appear</u> [as lust];

And <u>anoint your eyes</u> [with understanding] with eye salve [through reading], [so] that you may see.

19 As many as I love, I rebuke and chasten: be zealous therefore, and repent.

Rewards

Michelangelo, Libyan Sibyl.

20 Behold, I stand at the <u>door</u> [to the mind, at the cerebrum cortex], and knock:

If any man hear my voice, and open the door, I will come in to him,

"He that has an ear, let him hear ..."

And will sup with him [eating what Israel has chosen to eat], and he will eat [manna, living mass, atoms] with me. [2]

21 To him that overcomes I will grant [the privilege] to sit with me in my throne [the cerebellar cortex],

Even as I also overcame [the testing of the Z boson with photon], and am set down with [strong gravity] my Father in his throne [proton].

For the reader

22 He that has an ear, let him hear what [Atom Lambda] the [Holy] Spirit says to the churches [the minds of all people]. ✍

Revelation 3:14-22 KJV

2 Manna, particles of mass; any thing comprised of atoms, having life.

Balaam

1 And when Balaam [Jerusalem W^3] saw that it
pleased* the LORD to bless Israel, he went not,
as at other times, to seek for enchantments
[from photon in the electromagnetic field],
but he set his face toward the wilderness [the
mind of Atom Lambda, silence].

2 And Balaam lifted up his eyes, and he
saw Israel abiding in his tents [his intentions,
thinking] according to their tribes [the DNA or
RNA nucleobases]; and [Atom Lambda] the
spirit of God [strong Gravity] came upon him.
3 And he took up his parable [lesson plans],
and said, Balaam [W^3 boson] the son of Beor
[Jerusalem Z boson] has said, and [the W^3
boson] the man whose eyes are open has
said: 4 He has said, which heard the words
of God, which saw the vision of the Almighty,
falling into a trance, but having his eyes open:

Numbers 24:1-9 KJV

On Israel's Exploits

5 How goodly are your tents [intentions],
O Jacob [gluon strong nuclear], and your
tabernacles [your minds], O Israel [Judah,
Israel and Jerusalem]!

6 As the valleys, are they [gluons] spread
forth, as gardens by the river's side, as the
trees of lign aloes [self healing protons, gluons
and neutrons] which the LORD has planted,
and as cedar trees [e'phods] beside the
[hydrogen] waters.

7 He [Jacob] shall pour the water out of his
buckets [the Gentiles], and his seed [the quark
antiquark pairs] shall be in many waters [born
to Judah, Israel and Jerusalem],

And [Atom Lambda] his king shall be higher
than Agag [photon], and his [Israel's] kingdom
shall be exalted.

8 God brought him forth out of Egypt
[energy gyp, the uterus]; he [Israel gluon
strong nuclear] has, as it were, the strength
of a *unicorn* [as he is both light and mass, a
single vessel]:

He shall eat up the nations his enemies,
and shall break their bones, and pierce them
through with his arrows.

9 He couched, he lay down as a lion, and as
a great lion: Who shall stir him up?

Blessed is he that blesses you [Israel,
churches of Pergamos, Laodicea], and cursed
is he that curses you.

Numbers 24:1-9 KJV

Michelangelo, Last Judgment, Jonah, photon rules mankind

The brain of man is the throne of God, Atom Lambda. Whomever sits in the hindbrain and the forebrain rules the thoughts, actions the king, Judah, Israel, Jerusalem and the Gentiles. If life rules the energy pod, there is health, peace, longsuffering. If Jonah, photon electromagnetism death sits on the throne, there is destruction to mass, energy gyp, and forces are prevented from doing what they are created to do, move, repair, reason and learn.

Revelation 4

Who is Sitting on the Throne?

The Nature of Beasts

Beasts are kingdoms; each anatomical system, a principality. Atom Lambda commands all within the e'phod from the hindbrain. When we follow the will of Atom Lambda, the forces, mass and light follow us in the gravitational field. If we follow photon electromagnetism, our spirit, the radon Higgs boson, who generates our energy, mass and bosons of light, will follow him also and be destroyed in the fecal matter, drowned in urine. We have a responsibility to ensure our lives and the living mass within us.

1 After this I looked, and, behold, a door was opened in heaven [the brain]: and the first voice which I heard was, as it were, of a trumpet [Gabriel W^3] talking with me; which said, Come up here and I will show you things which must be hereafter*.

2 And immediately I was in the spirit [Atom Lambda]:

And, behold, a throne [the forebrain] was set in heaven [the brain]. And one [the electroweak interaction, SU(3), led by photon and followed by Z or W^3] sat on the throne.

Aurora Consurgens
15th Century
The electroweak interaction, SU(3), where photon leads and coerces the Z or W^3 bosons.

3 And he that sat [in the forebrain] was to look
upon like a jasper [a gluon] and a sardine stone [a Z boson]. And there was a rainbow [magnetism] round about the throne [the forebrain, in sight like unto an emerald [bile].

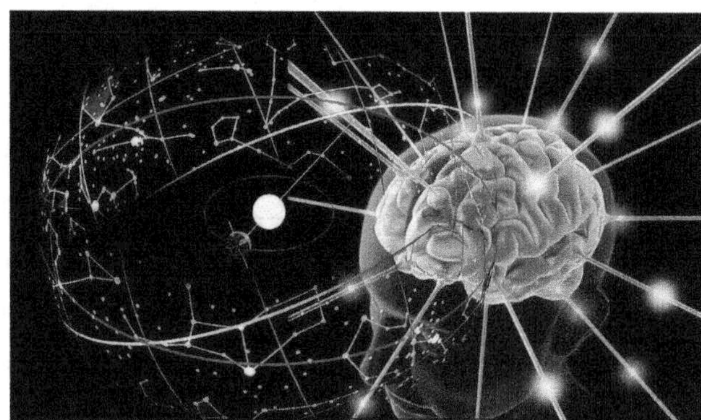

Heaven the Brain, the Mind

4 And round about the throne were four [forces: electroweak force, weak force, strong nuclear and strong Gravity].

And twenty seats [electricity and magnetism, as 20 is two, the zero is nought]:

And upon the seats I saw four [elders] sitting: [Z and W^1, W^2, W^3 bosons]; and twenty elders [two elders: photon carrying electricity conjoined to photon carrying magnetism];

[They were] clothed in white raiment [the light of the sun]. And on their heads they had crowns of gold [neurons racing through masses and disappearing, modes of communication].

FEAR IS SORCERY, MAGNETISM
[feer]
a distressing emotion aroused by photon electromagnetism of potential danger, pain often imagined and magnified, leading to apprehension, dismay.

"A throne was set in heaven, and one sat on the throne."

5 And out of the throne proceeded lightnings [electricity] and thunderings [strong Gravity] and voices [magnetism]:

And there were seven lamps of fire [minds] burning before the throne, which are the seven Spirits [atoms] of God [Atom Lambda]: Ephesus, Smyrna, Pergamos, Thyatira, Sardis, Philadelphia].

6 And before the throne there was a [hydrogen] sea of glass, [protons with gluons and neutrons] like unto crystal:

And in the midst of the throne, and round about the throne, were four beasts [in e'phods: Judah, Israel and Jerusalem and the Gentiles] full of eyes [bosons] before and [photons] behind.

7 And the first beast [is Israel with the behaviour of gluon strong nuclear] was like a lion,

And the second beast [is Jerusalem with the behaviour of gluon strong nuclear] like a calf,

And the third beast [is Judah having the behaviour of strong Gravity] had a face as a man,

And the fourth beast [is the Gentiles with the behaviour of electromagnetism] was like a flying eagle.

8 And the four beasts had each of them* six wings [of the six noble gases: helium, neon, argon, krypton, xenon, and radon], about him:

And they were full of eyes [lights, bosons, neurons and axon terminals] within:

And they rest not* day and night, saying, Holy, holy, holy, Lord God Almighty, which was, and is, and is to come.

9 And when those beasts [Judah, Israel and Jerusalem and the Gentiles] give glory and honour and thanks to [photon electromagnetism] him that sat on the throne [the forebrain], who *lives for ever and ever,*

10 The four and twenty elders [Z and W^1, W^2, W^3 bosons with photon carrying electricity conjoined to photon carrying magnetism] fall down before [Atom Lambda], him that sat on the throne, and worship him that *lives for ever and ever,* And cast their crowns [the crown of their heads] before the throne [in the hindbrain], saying,

11 You are worthy, [Atom Lambda strong Gravity] O Lord, to receive glory and honour and power: For you have created all things, and for your pleasure they are and were created. ✍

Revelation 4:1-11 KJV

Michelangelo, Last Judgment, Detail

The books are opened. Four angels blow their horns announcing the return of Christ, Atom Lambda. Atom Lambda holds the small book, physics that was recorded by strong Gravity before the world was made. The book contains the names and genetic codes of all atoms, their chemical makeup, of forces, mass and light that occurred before the singularity. No others may be created or destroyed. Gravity. Strong Gravity is he that made all things, from period one helium, proton through the singularity, the beginning of all things visible.

Michael (Israel gluon strong nuclear) holds the Book of Life, the genetic code for all people. It records the contributions to changes in the genetic code, whether good or bad. Four angels hover behind the Book of Life. Three of the four angels hold their horns waiting for a signal to wake the walking dead; the fourth partially hidden angel of the quark antiquark pair blows his horn.

Revelation 5

What's in that Book?

The Nature of Beasts

Beasts are kingdoms; each anatomical system, a principality. Atom Lambda commands all within the e'phod from the hindbrain. When we follow the will of Atom Lambda, the forces, mass and light follow us in the gravitational field. If we follow photon electromagnetism, our spirit, the radon Higgs boson, who generates our energy, mass and bosons of light, will follow him also and be destroyed in the fecal matter, drowned in urine. We have a responsibility to ensure our lives and the living mass within us.

1 And I saw in the right hand of [photon electromagnetism] him that sat on the throne [in the forebrain] a book written within and on the backside, sealed with seven seals [with the names of the seven churches].

2 And I saw [gluon strong nuclear] a strong angel proclaiming with a loud voice, Who is worthy to open the book, and to loose the seals thereof?

Who can read the prophecy?

11 All the future events in this vision are like a
sealed book to them. When you give it to those
who can read [having Z or W bosons], they will
say, "We can't read it because it is sealed." 12
When you give it to those who cannot read
[having a photon in the mind], they will say, "We
don't know how to read."

Isaiah 29:11-12 NLT

3 And no man in heaven, nor in earth, neither
under the earth, was able to open the book,
neither to look thereon. 4 And I wept much,
because no man was found worthy to open and
to read the book, neither to look thereon. 5 And
one of the elders said to me,

Weep not: behold, [Jesus Christ] the Lion of* the tribe of Juda [proton strong Gravity], [which is the Higgs boson] the Root of David [gluon strong nuclear], has prevailed to open the book, and to loose the seven seals [with the names of the seven churches] thereof.

6 And I beheld, and, lo, in the midst of the throne [the brain] and of the four beasts [consisting of atoms, forces, mass and light: Judah, Israel and Jerusalem, the Gentiles];

And in the midst of the elders [Z and W^1, W^2, W^3 bosons, with photon carrying electricity conjoined to photon carrying magnetism],

Stood a Lamb [Atom Lambda, just] as it had been slain;

Michelangelo, Jesus Christ
1508-1512

By the light of the Higgs boson, Atom Lambda in the hindbrain, Jesus Christ is drawn into the sun. He is risen.

Odours
[Thoughts]
An odour is a body of thought; that which one thinks; a product for mental consideration. A thought dissipates in the air almost as soon as it leaves the mind, just as an odour.

"The Lion of the tribe of Juda, the Root of David, hath prevailed to open the book ..."

[With Jesus Christ having] seven horns [voices] and seven eyes [bosons for understanding, wisdom], which are the seven Spirits [the radon Higgs bosons, souls in light, all wives of Atom Lambda], of God [strong Gravity];

[They are] sent forth into all the earth [every principality in all e'phods].

7 And he [Jesus Christ Atom Lambda] came and took the book out of the right hand of [photon electromagnetism], him that sat upon the throne.

8 And when he [Jesus Christ] had taken the book, the four beasts [Judah, Israel and Jerusalem, the Gentiles] and four and twenty elders [Z and W^1, W^2, W^3 bosons, with two photons] fell down before the Lamb [Atom Lambda], having every one of them harps [voices], and golden vials [brains] full of odours [considerations, perceptions, perspectives, all observed, heard by Atom Lambda], which are [thoughts], the prayers of saints.

9 And they sung a new song, saying, [Jesus Christ], you are worthy to take the book, and to open the seals thereof:

For you were slain: And [you] have redeemed us to God [Jesus Christ Atom Lambda] by your blood, [your deoxyribonucleic acid, that pulses] out of [the hearts of] every kindred [whose behaviours are as protons, gluon and neutron, quark-antiquark pairs], and tongue [language], and people [Judah, Israel and Jerusalem, the Gentiles], and nation [the Jewels or the Gentiles];

10 And [Jesus Christ] has made us kings [having crowns on our head] and priests [who think, like] unto [Atom Lambda] our God: and we [Judah, Israel and Jerusalem, the Gentiles] shall reign on the earth [in our kingdoms, our e'phods, making choices, by virtue of the crowns of our heads, even to the feet].

Blake, On the Morning
1803
Angels are overhead. Below is the house, the brain where Jesus and his parents lodge. Shepherds look on.

Distress in Labour

9 Now why dost thou cry out aloud? Is there no king [lighted crown] in thee? Is thy counsellor [Z boson] perished? For pangs have taken thee as a woman in travail. 10 Be in pain, and labour to bring forth, O daughter of Zion [Jerusalem], like a woman in travail: for now shalt thou go forth out of the city, and thou shalt dwell in the [electromagnetic] field, and thou shalt go even to Babylon [the uterus]; there shalt thou be delivered; there the LORD shall redeem thee from the hand of thine enemies.

Micah 4:9-10 KJV

11 And I beheld, and I heard the voice of many angels [bosons, lights] round about the throne and the beasts and the elders:

And the number of them [mass and light] was [infinite] ten thousand times ten thousand, and
thousands of thousands; 12 [They were] saying
with a loud voice,

Worthy is [Jesus Christ] the Lamb that was slain to receive power, and riches, and wisdom, and strength, and honour, and glory, and blessing.

13 And every creature which is in heaven, and on the earth, and under the earth, and such as are in the sea, and all that are in them, heard I saying,

Blessing, and honour, and glory, and power, be unto him [Jesus Christ, a Higgs boson] that sits upon the throne, and unto the Lamb [Atom Lambda] for ever and ever.

14 And [Judah, Israel and Jerusalem, the Gentiles], the four beasts said, Amen [all men].

And the four and twenty elders [Z and W^1, W^2, W^3 bosons, with two photons] fell down and worshiped him that lives for ever and ever. ✍

Revelation 5:1-14 KJV

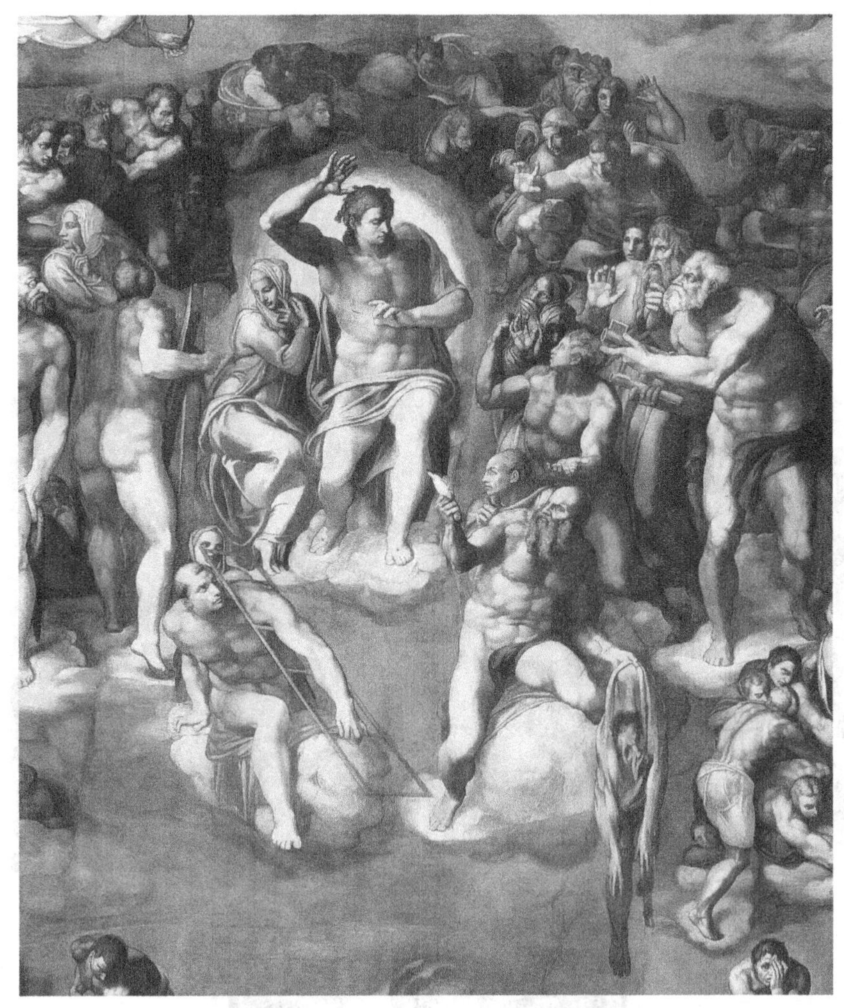

Michelangelo, Last Judgment, Detail

1508-1512

Jesus with the woman (proton). Jacob (gluon) holding his genetic ladder. Bartholomew (neutron) offering fecal matter and urine to eat. Jesus Christ and the woman are tested. They refuse.

Wheel of Fortune

Horses are forces. And forces are people, Judah, Israel and Jerusalem, the Gentiles. Our behaviour is such as the well documented behaviour of the four universal forces. Our crowns are our connection to Atom Lambda. Judah, at the top, wears a crown and carries the Higgs boson, his light, in his hand. By strong Gravity he rules with wisdom. His sceptre is as Atom Lambda. Israel is self-lit, gluon strong nuclear. Jerusalem exiles his crown when he follows his son, photon electromagnetism. The Gentiles have crowns, but they at a distance from the heads, as they are perpetrated by photon electromagnetism, merged with the Z boson. The Gentiles have no direct connection to Atom Lambda.

Revelation 6

Bella Omnium Contra Omnes

Punishment for the Jewels

Three Jewels, two Gentiles

Judah is my bow, and Israel is my arrow. Jerusalem is my sword, and like a warrior, I will brandish it against the Greeks.

Zechariah 9:13 NLT

1 And I saw when [Atom Lambda] the Lamb
opened one of the seals [the noble gas helium],
and I heard, as it were [strong Gravity whose
voice is] the noise of thunder, [and John heard]
one of the four beasts saying, Come and see.

Judah (strong Gravity), First Seal

2 And I saw, and behold a white horse [proton strong Gravity]: and [Judah], he that sat on him, had a bow; and a crown [a Higgs boson] was given to him: and he went forth conquering [increasing his knowledge, understanding, becoming wise], and [exploring more] to conquer.

Israel (strong nuclear), second Seal

3 And when he had opened the second seal
[the noble gas neon], I heard the second beast
[Israel] say, Come and see. 4 And there went
out another horse that was red [gluon strong
nuclear]: and power was given to him that
sat thereon to take peace from the earth [from
masses, people, unrestrained disorder], and that
they should kill one another: and there was given
unto him [electricity generating magnetism] a
great sword.

Jerusalem (electroweak-weak), third Seal

5 And when he had opened the third seal
[the noble gas argon], I heard [Jerusalem] the

Albrecht Dürer, Fortuna
1501-1503

The Z boson or W^3. balances on a ball, beguiling with praise or barking orders like a Sargent. Our responses are noted.

third beast say, Come and see. And I beheld, and lo a black horse [neutron electroweak-weak interaction]; and he that sat on him had a pair of balances in his hand.

6 And I heard a voice [Jerusalem, Z boson,
the disciplinarian] in the midst of the four beasts
say [in a complaining tone]:

A measure of wheat for a penny, and three measures of barley for a penny;

> **War between the nations: Jewels, Gentiles**
> The father shall be divided against the son, and the son against the father; the mother against the daughter, and the daughter against the mother; the mother in law against her daughter in law, and the daughter in law against her mother in law.
>
> Luke 12:53 KJV

"… He should take peace from the earth, and that they should kill one another …"

[And as W^3 boson, the teacher, he reminds]: And see thou hurt not the oil and the wine.

Gentiles (electromagnetism), fourth seal

7 And when he had opened the fourth seal [the noble gas krypton], I heard the voice of the fourth beast [the Gentiles electromagnetism] say, Come and see.

8 And I looked, and behold a pale horse [photon electromagnetism]: and his name that sat on him was Death [electricity], and Hell [magnetism] followed with him.

And power was given unto them [the Gentiles, quark-antiquark pairs, Z merged in photon with the W^3 boson at the ready] over the fourth part of the earth [the e'phods, the legs, feet and toes]: [His power is that of photon the deceiver] to kill with sword [electricity, just as Cain devised a plan in magnetism, and] killed his brother];

And with hunger [by eating the products of death: fecal matter and urine and menstrual blood comprised of matter, the living dead: rather than living masses: protons, gluons and neutrons];

And with death [electricity],

And with [violence between Judah, Israel and Jerusalem, the Gentiles] the beasts of the earth.

The souls beneath the altar, fifth seal

9 And when he had opened the fifth seal [the
noble gas xenon], I saw under the altar [under
the brain in the gravitational field, having been
transported into the electromagnetic field] the
souls [radon Higgs bosons, where memories are
recorded]. [These are] of them that were slain for
the word of God [for recognizing the truth and
refusing the deception]; And for the testimony
[concerning Atom Lambda who commands all
[energy, mass and light, the best and the worst],
which they [the souls] held: 10 And they cried
with a loud voice, saying,

How long, O Lord, holy and true? Do you not judge and avenge our blood on them that dwell on the earth?

11 And white robes [light from the sun] were given to every one of them; and it was said to them, that they should rest yet for a little season, until their fellow servants also and their brethren, that should be killed as* they were, should be fulfilled.

The Shaking, sixth seal

12 And I beheld when he had opened the sixth seal [the noble gas radon]. And, lo, there was a

Punishment for Israel

6 And he cast stones at David [Israel], and at all the servants of king David:
and all the people [protons, gluons and neutrons] and all the mighty men [gluon
strong nuclear and neutron] were on his right hand and [neutron] on his left. 7 And
thus said Shimei [Sardis] when he cursed, Come out, come out, thou bloody man
[Ourania], and thou man of Belial [Pandemos]: 8 The LORD hath returned upon
thee all the blood of the house of Saul [Sardis], in whose stead thou hast reigned;
and the LORD hath delivered the kingdom into the hand of Absalom [Sardis] thy
son: and, behold, thou art taken in thy mischief, because thou art a bloody man.

2 Samuel 16:6-8 KJV

great earthquake; and [Atom Lambda] the sun became black [magnetism] as sackcloth of hair, and the moon [Z or W^3] became as blood;

13 And [gluons] the stars of heaven fell unto the earth, even as a fig tree casteth her untimely figs, when she is shaken of a mighty wind.

14 And the heaven [the mind, emanating from the brain] departed as a scroll when it is rolled together;

And every mountain [forces: strong Gravity, strong nuclear and electroweak-weak force] and island [electricity and magnetism] were moved out of their places [in atoms and people, Jewels and the Gentiles].

15 And [Judah] the kings of the earth, and [Jerusalem] the great men, and [Israel] the rich men,

And the chief captains [protons],

And the mighty men [gluon strong nuclear],

And every bondman [the quark-antiquark
pairs], and every free man [neutron], hid
themselves in the dens [energy dens, in atoms]
and in the [anchored] rocks [radon Higgs bosons]
of the mountains [cerebellar cortex]; 16 And said
to the mountains and rocks,

Fall on us, and hide us from the face of [photon electromagnetism], him that sits on the throne [in the forebrain], and from the wrath of [Atom Lambda] the Lamb [in the hindbrain that rules the central nervous system]:

17 For the great day of his [Atom Lambda's] wrath is come; and who shall be able to stand? ✍

Revelation 6:1-17 KJV

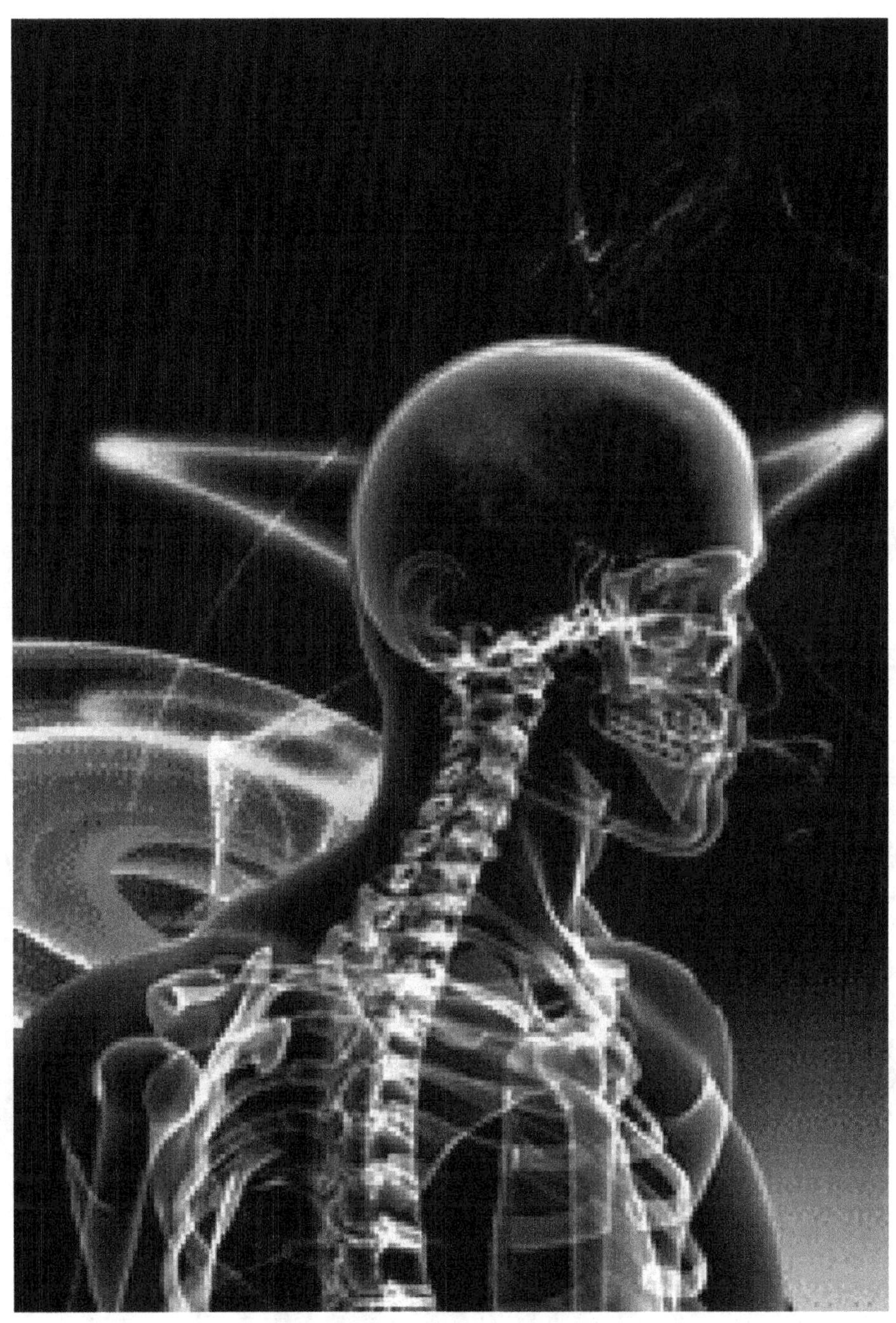

Rulers of the Brain and E'phods

The light at the forebrain is photon merged with the Z or W^3 boson, the electroweak unification. The light springing from the hindbrain is tat of Atom Lambda.

JESVS CHRIST
HE'S US CRYSTALIZED

Revelation 7

Seal of the Living God

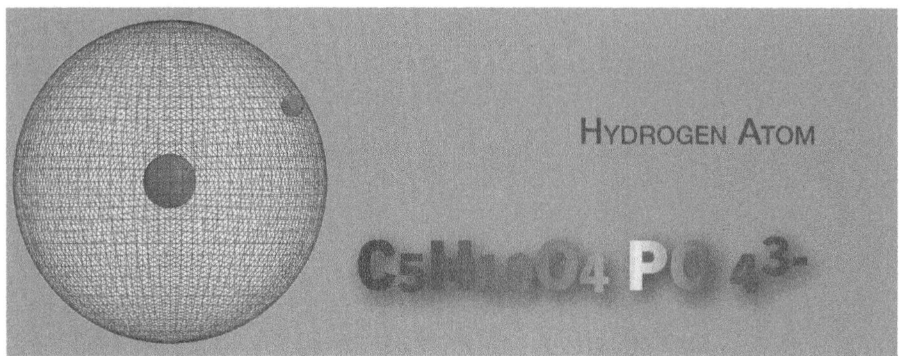

1 And after these things I saw four angels [the Higgs boson, gluon, Z boson or W^3 boson, light]; standing on the four corners of the earth, holding the four winds [strong Gravity, strong nuclear, electroweak-weak interaction, electromagnetism] of the earth [every e'phod], [so] that the wind [forces] should not blow on the earth [masses], nor on the [hydrogen] sea, nor on any tree [whether living in the gravitational field or dying in the electromagnetic field].

2 And I saw another angel [a gluon, the archangel Michael] ascending from the east [the midbrain,* having the [hydrogen] seal of [Atom Lambda strong Gravity] the living God:

MICHELANGELO, ARCHANGEL MICHEAL
1508-1512
Self-lit gluon, illustrated by the form of fire that is his hair.

And he [cried with a loud voice to the four
angels, to whom it was given to hurt the earth
and the sea, 3 Saying,

Hurt not the earth, neither the sea, nor the trees, till we have sealed the servants of our God in their foreheads [ousting the current ruler photon electromagnetism].

ONE HUNDRED AND FORTY AND FOUR THOUSAND

4 And I heard the number of them which were sealed:

And there were sealed an hundred [1] and forty [4] and four [4] thousand: [one God within: Atom Lambda in the hindbrain; four instances of mass and light: Judah, Israel and Jerusalem, the Gentiles] of all the tribes of the children of Israel; and the four universal forces: [strong Gravity, strong nuclear, electroweak-weak interaction, electromagnetism].

5 Of the tribe of Juda [Judah strong Gravity] were sealed twelve thousand.

Of the tribe of Reuben [Israel strong nuclear] were sealed twelve thousand.

Of the tribe of Gad [Jerusalem electroweak-weak] were sealed twelve thousand.

The Multitude before the Throne
All nations, and kindreds, and people, and tongues, stood before the throne. Atom Lambda sits in the cerebellar cortex, the hindbrain. All are born standing before the throne, the hindbrain.

"What are these which are arrayed in white robes?"

6 Of the tribe of Aser [the Gentiles electromagnetism] were sealed twelve thousand.

Of the tribe of Nepthalim [Judah strong Gravity] were sealed twelve thousand.

Of the tribe of Manasses [the Gentiles electromagnetism] were sealed twelve thousand.

7 Of the tribe of Simeon [Israel strong nuclear] were sealed twelve thousand.

Of the tribe of Levi [Jerusalem electroweak-weak] were sealed twelve thousand.

Of the tribe of Issachar [Judah strong Gravity] were sealed twelve thousand.

8 Of the tribe of Zabulon [Jerusalem electroweak-weak] were sealed twelve thousand.

Of the tribe of Joseph [Israel strong nuclear] were sealed twelve thousand.

Of the tribe of Benjamin [the Gentiles] were sealed twelve thousand.

Chant of the Multitude

9 After this, I beheld, and, lo, a great multitude [of atoms], which no man could number* [count], of all nations [the Jewels and the Gentiles], and kindreds [quark-antiquark pairs], and people [particles of mass, protons, gluons and neutrons],

Michelangelo, Centauro Machia
1492

and tongues [lights], stood before the throne; and before [Atom Lambda] the Lamb, [ruler of the central nervous system, back of the brain].

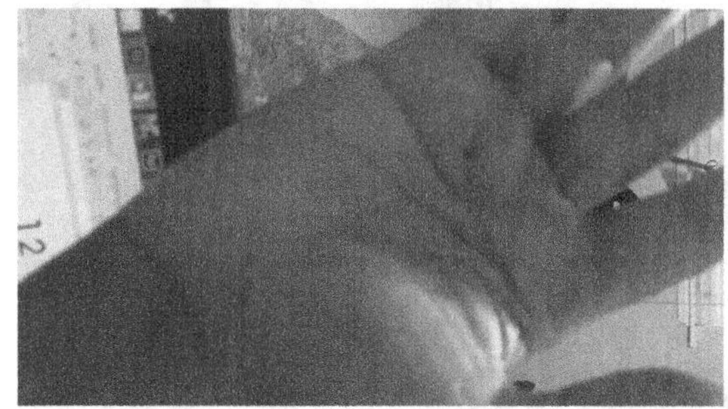

Palm of the Hand

[They are] clothed with white robes [light from the sun], and palms [visible lines] in their hands [begging for blessings that photon electromagnetism cannot deliver];

10 And cried with a loud voice, saying,

> "They shall hunger no more, neither thirst any more; neither* shall the sun light on them, nor any heat."

Salvation to our God [photon electromagnetism,
death and hell], which sits upon the throne [in
the forehead, defining the words and works,
emotions and reactions of all people]; and unto
[Atom Lambda in the hindbrain] the Lamb.

11 And all the angels [bosons, light] stood
round about the throne [in the hindbrain], and
about the elders [Z and W^1, W^2, W^3 bosons
with two photons]; and the four beasts, Judah,
Israel and Jerusalem, the Gentiles]: And [the

Blake, The Lord Answers Job out of a Whirlwind
1821

angels] fell before the throne on their faces, and
worshiped God, 12 Saying,

Amen: Blessing, and glory, and wisdom,
and thanksgiving, and honour, and power, and
might, be unto our God for ever and ever. Amen.

13 And one of the elders [a W^3 boson, the
teacher] answered, saying to me,

What are these which are arrayed in white
robes? And whence came they?

14 And I said unto him, Sir, you know.

And he said to me, These are they which
came out of great tribulation, and have washed
their robes, and made them* white in the blood
of the Lamb.

15 Therefore are they before the throne of
God, and serve him day and night in his temple:

And [Atom Lambda], he that sits on the
throne [the brain] shall dwell among them.

16 They shall hunger no more, neither thirst
any more; neither* shall [electricity, photon
from] the sun light upon them, nor [magnetism]
any heat [shall light upon the loins].

17 For [Jesus Christ] the Lamb which is in
the midst of the throne shall feed them [with
protons, gluons and neutrons],, and shall lead
them unto living fountains of waters: and God
[Atom Lambda] shall wipe away all tears from
their eyes. ✍

Revelation 7:1-17 KJV

Blake, Joy Comes in the Morning

Aurora Consurgens, Life in a Noble Gas

At the top of the circle is strong Gravity, who conceived the six noble gases through his urine excretions. Strong Gravity populated the universe with atoms. Atom Lambda is strong Gravity crystallized. On the left is gluon strong nuclear, neon, Ourania, the foundation of masses and movement. Argon electroweak force, krypton electromagnetism are next. The sun is xenon, W^3 boson, weak force. In this order, radon is the Higgs boson merged with gluon, the basis for living, for Adam and Eve. The last icon of the seven, is for gluon Pandemos, purveyor of war or peace by the command of Atom Lambda.

Revelation 8

Life: Four of Seven Seals

Incense

Used for aesthetic reasons, to enhance, lull. Used in therapy, meditation, and ceremony for dramatic effect. Also used as a simple deodorant or insectifuge (a substance or preparation for driving off insects).

The Seventh Seal

1 And when he had opened the seventh seal, there was silence in heaven [the mind for] about the space [spacetime] of half an hour [30, 3, the zero is naught; the three are the particles, the forces of life].

Seven Angels

2 And I saw the seven angels [radon Higgs bosons merged with gluons, one for each of the seven churches where we think in the e'phods where we live]: [These are they] which stood before [Atom Lambda] God; and to them were given seven trumpets [voices].

Prayers, Thoughts of the Saints

3 And another angel [Gabriel, Z or W^3 boson] came and stood at the altar [the heart, the blood], having a golden censer [electricity, Z boson];

And there was given to him much incense [magnetism, providing a false sense of peace], that he should offer it with the prayers of all saints upon the golden altar [the synaptically lit cerebrum cortex], which was before the throne [the cerebellar cortex].

4 And the smoke of the incense [the magnetism, deception, flattery], which came with the prayers of the saints, ascended up before God out of [Gabriel] the angel's hand.

5 And the angel [Gabriel] took the censer, and filled it with fire [electricity lighted neurons] of the altar [the brain], and cast it into the earth [the e'phods]:

And there were voices [by magnetism], and thunderings [by strong Gravity], and lightnings [by the electroweak-weak, electricity], and an earthquake [by strong nuclear].

Trumpets Announce the Beginning of Life

6 And the seven angels, which had the seven trumpets, prepared themselves to sound.

Proton, the Beginning of all Things Visible

7 The first angel sounded, and there followed hail [crystallization] and fire [electricity] mingled with blood, and they were cast upon the earth [proton, the hydrogen atom]: and the third part of trees [living mass] was burnt up, and all green grass [bile, matter] was burnt up.

Gluon, Noble Gas Neon, DNA, Eukaryote

8 And the second angel sounded, and, as it

The Multitude before the Throne
All nations, and kindreds, and people, and tongues, stood before the throne. Atom Lambda sits in the cerebellar cortex, the hindbrain. All are born standing before the throne, the hindbrain.

"The name of the star is called Wormwood."

were, a great mountain [strong Gravity] burning with fire [electricity] was cast into the [hydrogen] sea:

And the third part of the [hydrogen] sea became blood;

9 And the third part of the creatures which were in the [hydrogen] sea, and had life, died;

And the third part of the ships [the transport system in the blood] were destroyed.

Neutron, Noble Gas Argon, RNA, Archaic

10 And the third angel sounded, and there fell a great star [gluon] from heaven [Higgs boson], burning as it were a lamp [a boson], and it fell upon the third part of the rivers [neutron Z boson], and upon the fountains of waters

Michelangelo, Last Judgment Detail
1508-1512
The judge strikes with a paddle, electricity; the teacher wrapped in the serpent tests, tempts with magnetism.

[neutron W^3 boson];

11 And the name of the star is called Wormwood [who like termites on wood, eats flesh and masses from the inside out]: and the third part of the waters became* wormwood [as bile]; and many men died of the waters, because they were made bitter [negative, having little good to say; producing nothing of value for the living].

Photon, Noble Gas Krypton, Prokaryote

12 And the fourth angel sounded, and the third part of the sun [proton] was smitten, and [neutron] the third part of the moon, and [gluon] the third part of the stars; so as the third part of them was darkened;

And the day shone not for a third part of it, and the night likewise.

Prophecy

13 And I beheld, and heard an angel flying through the midst of heaven, saying with a loud voice, Woe, woe, woe, to the inhabiters of the earth [the e'phods] by reason of the other voices of the trumpet of the three angels, which are yet to sound! ✍

Revelation 8:1-13 KJV

Blake, Emanation of the Giant Albion

Head in hands when discovering the truth. Erdman p. 184.

Revelation 9

Last Three Seals

The Constant

For I [Atom Lambda] am the LORD, I change not; therefore ye sons of Jacob [Judah, Israel and Jerusalem, the Gentiles] are not consumed.

Malachi 3:6 KJV

Change is in the Air

1 And the fifth angel [W^3 boson] sounded, and I saw [photon] a star fall from heaven [the sun] unto the earth: and to him was given the key of the bottomless pit [the colon, bladder and bowels].
2 And he opened the bottomless pit; and there arose a smoke [gases] out of the pit, as the smoke of a great furnace; and the sun [proton] and the air [gluon] were darkened by reason of the smoke of the pit.

Menses, a Rise in magnetic Power

3 And there came out of the smoke locusts [bacteria] upon the earth [the e'phod]: and unto them was given power [electricity], as the scorpions of the earth have power.

4 And it was commanded them that they should not hurt the grass of the earth, neither any green thing, neither any tree [gamete seeds to bear the seven churches]; but only [hurt] those men [people] which have not [the truth] the seal of God [Atom Lambda] in their foreheads [brains, minds].

5 And to them [the locusts] it was given that they should not kill them, but that they should be tormented five [days all] months [during the childbearing years]: and their torment was as the torment of a scorpion when he strikes a man.

Tormented by Menstruating Women

6 And in those days [of highly sensitive emotional attacks] shall men seek death, and shall not find it; and shall desire to die, and death [electromagnetism] shall flee from them.

7 And the shapes of the locusts were like unto horses prepared unto battle; and on their heads were as it were crowns like gold, and their faces were as the faces of men [women].

8 And they had hair [moved by magnetism] as the hair of women, and their teeth were as the teeth of lions [ready to eat you alive].

9 And they had breastplates [rib cages], as it were breastplates of iron [electricity];

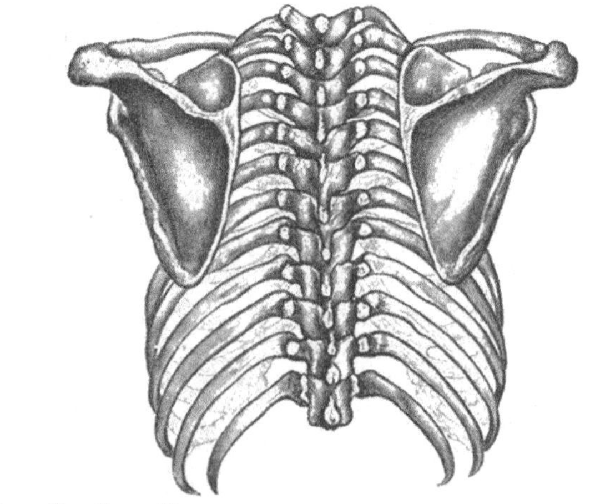

Gray, Rib Cage, Breastplate

Removing Cain from DNA

What was stretched to accommodate Cain will shrink when Sardis is removed.

"They had a king over them, which is the angel of the bottomless pit ..."

And the sound of their wings [voices] was as the sound of chariots [clattering], of many horses running to battle.

10 And they had tails [geni-tails] like unto scorpions, and there were stings [fungal and sexually transmitted diseases] in their tails [bladder and bowels]: and their power was to hurt men five [days, all] months.

Blake, Apollyon
Circa 1815
Apollyon, gluon Pandemos, holds electromagnetism, the serpent, while gluon Ourania escapes.

11 And they had a king over them [gluon strong nuclear Pandemos], which is the angel of the bottomless pit [the reproductive system that sits in th midst of the bladder and bowels]; whose name in the Hebrew tongue is Abaddon, but in the Greek tongue has his name Apollyon [gluon strong nuclear, Israel Pandemos].

12 One woe is past; and, behold, there come two woes more hereafter*.

Four angels loosed to Slay

13 And the sixth angel [a radon Higgs boson] sounded, and I heard a voice from the four horns [Judah, Israel and Jerusalem, the Gentiles] of the golden altar [the cerebrum cortex] which is before [the throne in the cerebellar cortex where sits Atom Lambda], God,

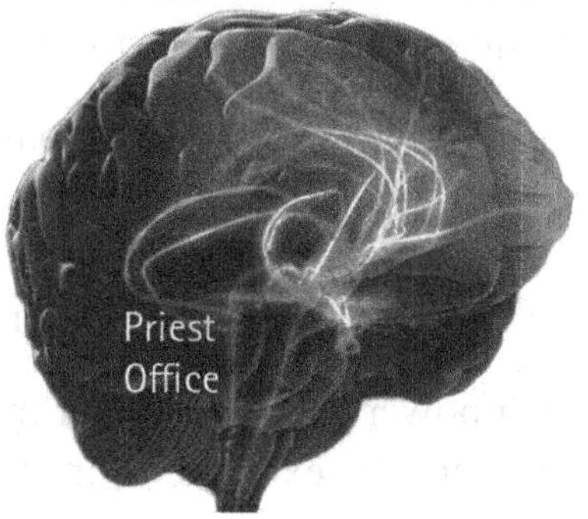

Ribbed section below is the cerebellar cortex is the Priest's Office, from where understanding emanates.

14 Saying to the sixth angel which had the trumpet, Loose the four angels which are bound in the great river Euphrates [the digestive system, from the tip of the tongue to the bladder and bowels].

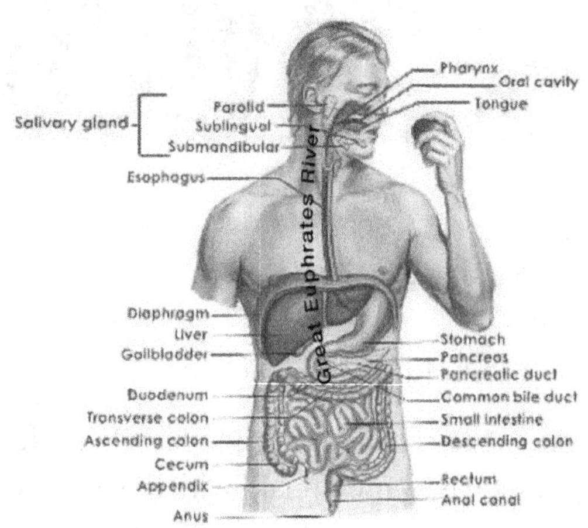

Great River Euphrates

15 And the four angels were loosed, which were prepared for an hour, and a day, and a month, and a year, for to slay the third part of men.

16 And the number of the army of the horsemen were two hundred thousand thousand: and I
heard the number of them. 17 And thus I saw
the horses in the vision, and them that sat on them, having breastplates of fire [blood], and of jacinth [electricity], and brimstone [magnetism]:

And the heads of the horses [forces] were as the heads of lions; and out of their mouths issued fire and smoke and brimstone.

18 By these three was the third part of men killed, by the fire [contaminated blood], and by the smoke [toxic gases], and by the brimstone [magnetism], which issued out of their mouths.

19 For their power [to kill] is [what they put] in their mouth, and [the excrement] in their tails:

For their tails were like unto serpents [photons], and had heads [photon carrying electricity and photon carrying magnetism], and with them they do hurt.

Nuremberg Chronicles
The conjoined heads of photon electromagnetism.

20 And the rest of the men which were not killed by these plagues yet repented not of the works of their hands, that they should not worship devils, and idols of gold, and silver, and brass, and stone, and of wood: which neither can see, nor hear, nor walk:

21 Neither repented they of their murders, nor of their sorceries, nor of their fornication, nor of their thefts. ✍

Only one God, Atom Lambda

1 "But now, listen to me, Jacob my servant, Israel
my chosen one. 2 The LORD who made you and
helps you says: Do not be afraid, O Jacob, my
servant, O dear Israel, my chosen one. 3 For I will
pour out water to quench your thirst and to irrigate
your parched fields. And I will pour out my Spirit
on your descendants, and my blessing on your
children. 4 They will thrive like watered grass, like
willows on a riverbank.

5 Some will proudly claim, 'I belong to the
LORD.' Others will say, 'I am a descendant of
Jacob.' Some will write [Atom Lambda] the LORD
's name on their hands and will take the name of
Israel as their own."

6 This is what the LORD says—Israel's King
and Redeemer, the LORD of Heaven's Armies: "I
am the First and the Last; there is no other God.
7 Who is like me? Let him step forward and prove
to you his power. Let him do as I have done since
ancient times when I established a people and
explained its future. 8 Do not tremble; do not be
afraid. Did I not proclaim my purposes for you long
ago [in proton, gluon and neutron]? You are my
witnesses—is there any other God? No! There is
no other Rock—not one!"

9 How foolish are those who manufacture idols.
These prized objects are really worthless. The
people who worship idols don't know this, so they
are all put to shame. 10 Who but a fool would make
his own god— an idol that cannot help him one bit?
11 All who worship idols will be disgraced along
with all these craftsmen—mere humans— who
claim they can make a god. They may all stand
together, but they will stand in terror and shame. 12
The blacksmith stands at his forge to make a sharp
tool, pounding and shaping it with all his might.
His work makes him hungry and weak. It makes
him thirsty and faint. 13 Then the wood-carver
measures a block of wood and draws a pattern
on it. He works with chisel and plane and carves it
into a human figure. He gives it human beauty and
puts it in a little shrine. 14 He cuts down cedars; he
selects the cypress and the oak; he plants the pine
in the forest to be nourished by the rain. 15 Then
he uses part of the wood to make a fire. With it
he warms himself and bakes his bread. Then—yes,
it's true—he takes the rest of it and makes himself
a god to worship! He makes an idol and bows
down in front of it! 16 He burns part of the tree to
roast his meat and to keep himself warm. He says,
"Ah, that fire feels good."

17 Then he takes what's left and makes his god:
a carved Idol [of a so-called saint, Mary, Jesus]!
He falls down in front of it, worshiping and praying
to it. "Rescue me!" he says. "You are my god!"
18 Such *stupidity and ignorance*! Their eyes are
closed, and they cannot see. Their minds are shut,
and they cannot think. 19 The person who made the
idol never stops to reflect, "Why, it's just a block of
wood! I burned half of it for heat and used it to
bake my bread and roast my meat. How can the
rest of it be a god? Should I bow down to worship
a piece of wood?" 20 The poor, deluded fool feeds
on ashes. He trusts something that can't help him
at all. Yet he cannot bring himself to ask, "*Is this
idol that I'm holding in my hand a lie*?"

21 "Pay attention, O Jacob, for you are my
servant, O Israel. I, the LORD, made you, and I
will not forget you. 22 I have swept away your sins
like a cloud. I have scattered your offenses like the
morning mist. Oh, *return to me, for I have paid the
price to set you free.*"

23 Sing, O heavens, for the LORD has done
this wondrous thing. Shout for joy, O depths of the
earth! Break into song, O mountains and forests
and every tree! For the LORD has redeemed Jacob
and is glorified in Israel. 24 This is what the LORD
says— your Redeemer and Creator: "I am the
LORD, who made all things. I alone stretched out
the heavens. Who was with me when I made the
earth? 25 I expose the false prophets as liars and
make fools of fortune-tellers. I cause the wise to
give bad advice, thus proving them to be fools.
26 But I carry out the predictions of my prophets!
By them I say to Jerusalem, 'People will live here
again,' and to the towns of Judah, 'You will be
rebuilt; I will restore all your ruins!' 27 When I speak
to the rivers and say, 'Dry up!' They will be dry.

28 When I say of Cyrus, 'He is my shepherd,' he
will certainly do as I say. He will command, 'Rebuild
Jerusalem'; he will say, 'Restore the Temple.'"

Isaiah 44:1-28 NLT

Michelangelo, Last Judgment (detail)

1508-1512

Eve, her face in Adam's genitalia, consuming semen knitted from fecal matter and urine. The secret is one of the mysteries in the contents of the small scroll that John was given to eat. This act constitutes idol worship; this worship is compelled by photon electromagnetism.

Revelation 10

The Small Scroll

Thunders

The voice of [Atom Lambda] the LORD is upon the waters: [strong Gravity] the God of glory thunders: [Atom Lambda] the LORD is upon many [hydrogen] waters [mass and matter, life and death, Jewels and Gentiles].

Psalm 29:3 KJV

1 Then I saw another mighty angel [Apollyon,
gluon strong nuclear] coming down from
heaven, surrounded by a [gluon] cloud, with
a rainbow [magnetism] over his head. His face
shone like the sun, and his feet were like pillars
of fire.

Aurora Consurgens, Two sides of gluon strong nuclear
15th Century

As the captain of the immunological armies, the warrior with the head of gold carries electricity. He protects proton, Atom Lambda, life. The female, riding the crow with the legs of a lion, is the keeper of the gametes as he rules the reproductive system.

2 And in his hand was a small scroll that had
been opened.

He stood with his right foot on the [hydrogen] sea and his left foot on the land [hydrogen mass of the reproductive system, particles as gametes waiting for seminal fertilization, incubated by the warmth of the outlying excrement].

3 And he gave a great shout like the roar of a
lion. And when he shouted, the seven thunders
[seven variations of light created by strong
Gravity] answered. 4 When the seven thunders
spoke, I was about to write. But I heard a voice
from heaven saying, "Keep secret what the seven
thunders said, and do not write it down."

5 Then the angel I saw standing on the
[hydrogen] sea and on [protons, gluons and
neutrons] the land, raised his right hand toward
heaven. 6 He swore an oath in the name of [Atom
Lambda, the beginning of all things visible, the
first singularity] the one who lives forever and
ever, who created the heavens and everything in
them, the earth [e'phods] and everything in it,
and the [electromagnetic] sea [excrement] and
everything in it. He said, "There will be no more
delay.

Laodicea, the Seventh Angel Speaks

7 When the seventh angel blows his trumpet,
God's mysterious plan will be fulfilled. It will
happen just as he announced it to his servants
the prophets."

8 Then the voice from heaven spoke to me
again:

Electromagnetism

The conjoined electromagnetic force projects electromagnetic fields, electric fields, magnetic fields, and light.

Wherefore they are no more twain, but one flesh. What therefore God hath joined together, let not man put asunder.

Matthew 19:6 KJV

"There will be no more delay. ... God's mysterious plan will be fulfilled."

"Go and take the open scroll from the hand of the angel who is standing on the sea and on
the land." 9 So I went to the angel and told him
to give me the small scroll.

"Yes, take it and eat it," he said. "It [magnetism emanating from the dead or dying matter] will be sweet as honey in your mouth, but it will turn sour [striking with electricity] in your stomach!"

10 So I took the small scroll [magnetism, containing all the contamination and toxicity afforded by death from the electromagnetic field] from the hand of the angel, and I ate it! It was sweet in my mouth, but when I swallowed it, it turned sour in my stomach.

11 Then I was told, "You must prophesy again about many peoples [particles of mass and matter], nations [Jewels and Gentiles], languages [life or death], and kings [Judah, Israel and Jerusalem, the Gentiles]." ✍

Revelation 10:1-11 KJV

12 Take heed to yourself, lest you [are tricked and] make a covenant with [photons, Z boson] the inhabitants of the land [mass and matter that comprises you] wherever you go, lest it be [ripe] for a snare [perpetrated in the mind and the reproduction organs], in the midst of you:
13 But you [Judah, Israel and Jerusalem, the Gentiles] shall destroy their altars [the blood], break their images [their handmade gods, talisman, beads], and cut down their groves
[so that they will no longer reproduce]: 14 For
you shall worship no other god: for [Atom Lambda] the LORD, whose name is *Jealous, is a jealous God*:

15 Lest you make a covenant with [the Gentiles] the inhabitants of the land, and they go a whoring after their gods, and do sacrifice unto their gods, and one call you, and you eat of his sacrifice [semen];

16 And you take of their daughters unto your sons, and their daughters go a whoring after their gods, and make your sons go a whoring after their gods.

Exodus 34:12-16 KJV

Michelangelo, Last Judgment (detail)

Contents of an atom: Atom Lambda and all that is within him: Judah (proton, a male and a separate female); Israel (gluon with his DNA ladder); and Jerusalem (neutron shedding his electroweak skin for the mild mannered weak force).

Revelation 11

Two Witnesses to Atom's Power

Destruction of the Gentiles

The lion is come up from his thicket, and the destroyer of the Gentiles is on his way; he is gone forth from his place to make thy land desolate; and thy cities shall be laid waste, without an inhabitant.

Jeremiah 4:7 KJV

1 And there was given me a reed [the weak force]
like unto a rod [the electroweak force (merged as
one light, SU(3)]:

CHIMERA
Ca. 350-340 BC
Head of a lion (Z boson), head of a gazelle (W^3 boson), head of a snake (photon) on the tail.

And the angel stood, saying, Rise, and measure the temple [the brain] of God, and the altar [the blood flowing through the heart], and them that worship therein*.

2 But the court [extending from the forebrain]
which is without [outside] the temple, leave out, and measure it not; For it is given to the Gentiles:

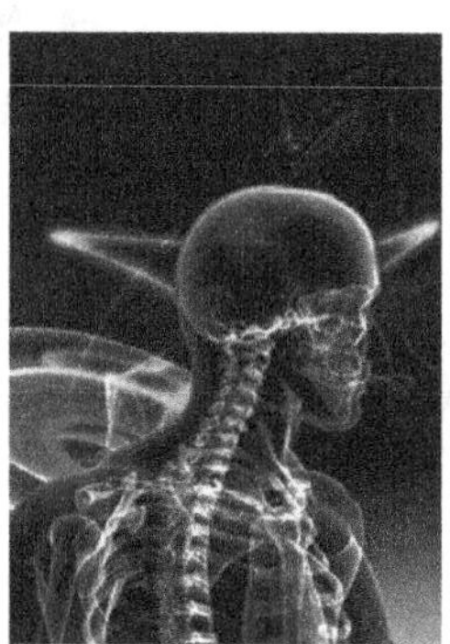

THE OUTER COURTYARD EMANATING FROM THE FOREBRAIN

And the holy city shall they tread under foot [for] forty [four: Higgs boson, gluon, Z boson or W^3] and two [photon carrying electricity conjoined to photon carrying magnetism]; months [spacetime].

Two Witnesses

3 And I will give power unto my two witnesses,
and they shall prophesy a thousand two hundred and threescore days, clothed in sackcloth.

4 These are the two olive trees, and the two
candlesticks standing before the God of the
earth. 5 And if any man* will hurt them, fire
proceeds out of their mouth, and devours their enemies: and if any man will hurt them, he must in this manner be killed.

6 These have power to shut heaven, that it
rain* not in the days of their prophecy: and have

Cyrus, Constance
C-yr us: See you're us.

Behold, my servant [Constance, Cyrus] shall deal prudently; He shall be exalted and extolled, and be very high.

Isaiah 52:13 KJV

"These have power to shut heaven, that it rain* not ..."

power over waters to turn them to blood, and to smite the earth with all plagues, as often as they will.

Michelangelo, Last Judgment (Detail)
1508-1512
Jesus Christ and the woman who fought the dragon.

7 And when they shall have finished their testimony, [photon electromagnetism] the beast that ascends out of the bottomless pit shall make war against them, and shall overcome them, and kill them.

Aurora Consurgens, Light in the brain severed from the dead
15th Century
Death is photon electricity, the head and photon magnetism, the tail.

8 And their dead bodies shall lie in the street of the great city, which spiritually is called Sodom [electricity, making waste, fecal matter] and Egypt [e-gypt, energy gyp, magnetism lacks energy], where also [the Higgs boson that is Jesus Christ] our Lord was crucified.

9 And they of the people [protons, gluons and neutrons] and kindreds [quark-antiquarks] and tongues [life or death] and nations [Jewels and the Gentiles] shall see their dead bodies [through the light of] three days [Judah, Israel and Jerusalem] and [Ephesus] a half, [of the conjoined pair]; And [these three and a half] shall not suffer their dead bodies to be put in graves [in photons, quarks with antiquarks in the electromagnetic field].

Made in Atom Lambda's Image

So God created man in his own image, in the image of God created he him; male and female created he them.

Genesis 1:27 KJV

10 And they that dwell upon the earth shall rejoice over them, and make merry, and shall send gifts one to another; because these two prophets tormented them [with truth] that dwelt on the earth.

11 And after three [Judah, Israel and Jerusalem] days [lights of life] and an half [Ephesus (life, of the conjoined pair (*not Sardis, death*)], [the Higgs boson] the Spirit of life from God [Atom Lambda] entered into them.

And [by the force of strong Gravity] they stood upon their feet;

And great fear fell upon them which saw them.

12 And they heard a great voice from heaven [the brain, Atom Lambda, the sun] saying unto them, Come up here. And they ascended up to heaven in a [gluon] cloud; And [Z boson and photon], their enemies beheld them.

The Shaking

13 And the same* hour was there a great earthquake [by gluon strong nuclear]: And the tenth part [where 10 is all, complete] of [Jerusalem] the city [at the forehead] fell, and in the earthquake were slain* of men seven [churches] thousand: and the remnant [Judah, Israel and Jerusalem, Ephesus] were affright, and gave glory to the God of heaven.

14 The second woe is past; and, behold, the third woe cometh quickly.

The Seventh Angel

15 And [gluon] the seventh angel sounded; and there were great voices in heaven, saying,

The kingdoms [e'phods of Judah, Israel and Jerusalem] of this world are become the kingdoms of [Atom Lambda], our LORD, and of his Christ;

And he [Atom Lambda] shall reign for ever and ever.

16 And the four [Higgs, gluon, Z boson and W3 boson] and twenty [two: photon carrying electricity conjoined with photon carrying magnetism] elders, which sat *before* God [in the forebrain; whose throne is the hindbrain] on their seats, fell upon their faces, and worshiped God [Atom Lambda, strong Gravity],

17 Saying, We give you thanks, O Lord God Almighty, which are, and was, and are to come; because you hast taken to thee thy great power, and have reigned.

18 And the nations were angry, and [now] your wrath is come: And the time of the dead [is

We are Atoms, Adams

And Adam lived an hundred and thirty years, and begat a son in his own likeness, after his image; and called his name Seth.

Genesis 5:3 KJV

"And he shall reign for ever and ever!"

come], that they should be judged:

And [the time is come] that you should give reward to your servants the prophets [Judah, Israel and Jerusalem], and to the saints [in whose image the prophets are made, protons, gluons and neutrons], and them [the Gentiles] that fear your name; small and great; and should destroy them which destroy the earth.

19 And the temple of God [the mind] was opened in heaven [the brain], and there was

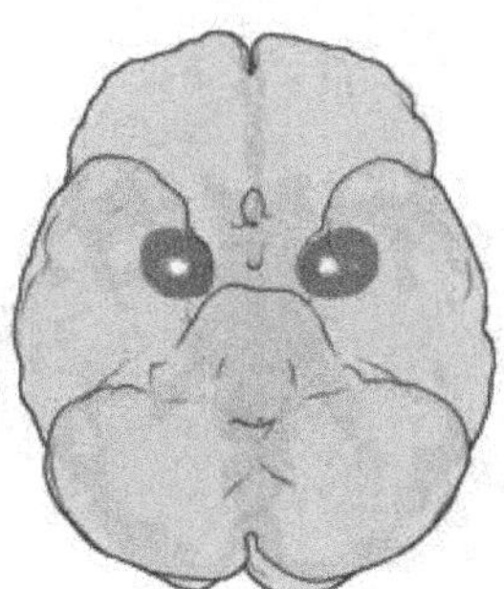

Amygdala at the mid brain, ruled by gluon strong nuclear

seen in his temple, the ark [of the midbrain, the amygdala][1] of his testament:

And [from strong Gravity] there were lightnings [electricity], and voices [weak-electroweak-weak, magnetism], and thunderings [strong Gravity], and an earthquake [gluon strong nuclear], and great hail [crystallization, Atom Lambda]. ✍

Revelation 11:1-19 KJV

1 Memory, decision-making, and emotional reactions.

Constance, the Woman who Fought the Dragon

The sun is Atom Lambda, the light emanating from the brain. The star at the shoulder is gluon strong nuclear, the strength. The pearl as moon beneath her feet is neutron, the electroweak-weak interaction

Revelation 12

The Second Witness

The Great Deception

Because, even because they have seduced my people, saying, Peace; and there was no peace; and one built up a wall, and, lo, others daubed it with untempered mortar [fecal matter and urine]: Say unto them which daub it with untempered mortar, that it shall fall ...

Ezekiel 13:10-11 KJV

1 And there appeared a great wonder in
heaven; a woman clothed with the sun [within
Atom Lambda], and the moon [electroweak-
electromagnetism-weak force] under her feet,
and upon her head a crown of twelve [gluon]
stars: 2 And she being with child cried, travailing
in [the] birth [of the mystery of the revelation],
and pained [tortured] to be delivered.

3 And there appeared another wonder in heaven; and behold [gluon strong nuclear] a great red dragon, having seven heads [gametes of the seven churches: Ephesus, Smyrna, Pergamos, Thyatira, Sardis, Philadelphia and Laodicea] and ten horns [a complete set of voices], and seven crowns [boson, gluon, particles of light] upon his heads.

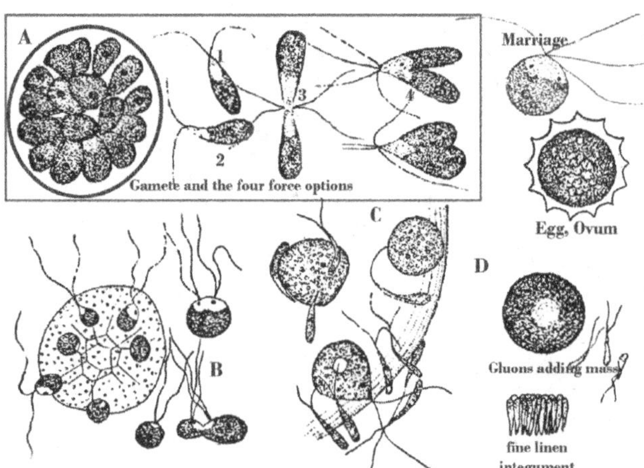

Chart of Gametes activity from gluon to delivery

4 And his tail drew the third part of the stars of heaven [one-third of proton, of gluon and neutron to make room for the Gentiles]; And did cast them [the quark-antiquark seeds] to the earth [as gametes, seeds to be reproduced by Jewels and the Gentiles]:

And the dragon stood before the woman which was ready to be delivered, for to devour her child as soon as it was born.

5 And she brought forth a man child [a proton], who was to rule all nations with [electricity] a rod of iron: And her child was caught up to [Atom Lambda] God, and to his throne [the sun].

6 And the woman fled into the wilderness [the gravitational field], where she has a place prepared of God, that they should feed her there [for] a thousand [one God, Atom Lambda]; two hundred [two bosons of life: Higgs, gluon]; And threescore [three] days [bosons, lights: Z boson, photon, W^3 bosons].

War in Heaven

7 And there was war in heaven: Michael
[gluon strong nuclear, Pandemos, electricity]
and his [immunological] angels fought against
the dragon [photon electromagnetism]; And the
dragon fought and his [contaminated bodies]
angels, 8 And prevailed not; neither was their

Cyrus, Constance
C-yr us: See you're us.

Behold, my servant [Constance, Cyrus] shall deal prudently; He shall be exalted and extolled, and be very high.

Isaiah 52:13 KJV

"Now is come salvation, and strength, and the kingdom of our God ..."

place found any more in heaven [the brain,
mind]. 9 And [photon electromagnetism] the
great dragon was cast out, that old serpent, called
the Devil [electricity], and Satan [magnetism],
which deceives the whole world: he was cast
out [of the sun] into the earth, and his angels
[photons] were cast out with him.

10 And I heard a loud voice saying in heaven,
Now is come salvation [strong Gravity], and
strength [strong nuclear], and the kingdom
of our God [electroweak-weak force], and the
power [electromagnetism] of his Christ:

For the accuser of our brethren is cast down, which accused them before our God day and night.

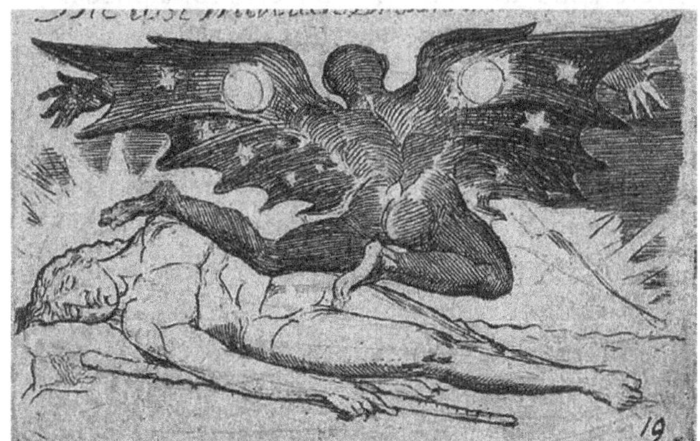

Aurora Consurgens, SU(3) the Accuser
The spectre is photon electromagnetism, his foot on the reproductive organs, the second mind with its own agenda.

11 And they overcame him [the accuser] by
[DNA evidence] the [pure] blood of the Lamb
[Atom Lambda], and by the word [the truth] of
their testimony; And they loved not their lives
to the death [trading truth for deception, Atom
Lambda (life) for photon (death)].

12 Therefore* rejoice, ye heavens, and ye that
dwell in them. Woe to the inhabiters of the
earth and of the sea! For the devil [electricity] is
come down to you, having great wrath, because
he knows that he has but a short time [before
electricity dies, becoming ashes].

13 And when the dragon saw that he was
cast unto the earth [beneath the masses], he
persecuted the woman which brought forth
[proton] the man child. 14 And to the woman was
given two wings [gluons] of a great eagle [Atom
Lambda], that she might fly into the wilderness
[the gravitational field], into her place [within
Atom Lambda], where she is nourished for a
time* [a lifetime], And times [the times, joy of
her life],

A Time, Times and Half a time

And half a time [the period just prior to death,
during the liquefaction of crystalline mass],
from the face of the serpent. 15 And the serpent
cast out of his mouth [waste] water, as a flood
after the woman [drenching her head and chest,
legs], that he might cause her to be carried away
of the flood of illnesses, one after another.

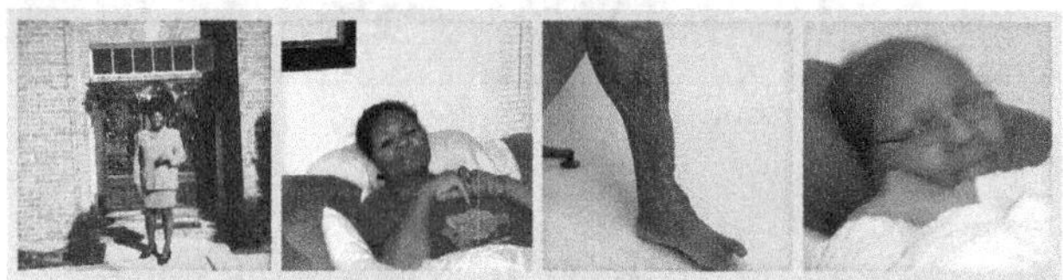

Steady Decline in Health by the exploits of photon

16 And the earth [atoms] helped [Constance]
the woman [Cyrus],

And the earth [protons, gluons and neutrons] opened her mouth, and swallowed up the flood which the dragon cast out of his mouth.

Triniti, Illustration of woman and dragon

17 And the dragon was wroth with the woman,
and went to make war with the remnant of her
seed [Judah, Israel and Jerusalem, the Gentiles],
which keep the commandments [the physical
laws of Atom Lambda, as written in the Ark of
the Covenant, at the midbrain] of God,

And have the testimony of Jesus Christ [which
he left as the four gospels, on for each of the
four: three Jewels and two conjoined Gentiles].
18 [Silence in heaven, discussions on earth.] ✍

Revelation 12:1-18 KJV

Have You Seen These Abominations?

12 Then said he unto me [Ezekiel], Son of man,
have you seen what [Judah, Israel and Jerusalem
and the Gentiles] the ancients of the house of
Israel do in the dark, every man in the chambers
of his imagery [consuming fecal matter and
urine and menstrual blood]? For they say, The
LORD sees us not; the LORD hath forsaken the
earth. 13 He [Atom Lambda] said also unto me,
Turn thee yet again, and thou shalt see greater
abominations that they do.

14 Then he brought me to the door of the
gate of the LORD'S house, which was toward
the north [the electromagnetic field, bladder and
bowels]; and, behold, there sat women weeping
for Tammuz [the loss of the unstable Gentiles
children]. 15 Then said he unto me, Hast thou
seen this, O son of man?

Turn thee yet again, and thou shalt see greater
abominations than these. 16 And he brought me
into the inner court [red nucleus and substantia
nigra] of the LORD'S house [the brain], and,
behold, at the door of the temple of the LORD,
between the porch and the altar, were about five
Smyrna, Pergamos, Thyatira, Philadelphia and
Laodicea]and twenty [two, Ephesus and Sardis],
men with their backs toward the temple of the
LORD, and their faces toward the east; and they
worshiped the sun [photon electromagnetism]
toward the east [toward the midbrain].

17 Then he said unto me, Hast thou seen this,
O son of man? Is it a light thing to the house of
Judah that they commit the abominations which
they commit here? For they have filled the land
[e'phods] with violence [by their food source],
and have returned to provoke me to anger: and,
lo, they put the branch [the reproductive organs]
to their nose. 18 Therefore will I also deal in fury:
mine eye shall not spare, neither will I have pity:
and though they cry in mine ears with a loud
voice, yet will I not hear them.

Ezekiel 8:12-18 KJV

Constance, the Man with the Writing Case

1 He [Atom Lambda] cried also in mine ears
with a loud voice, saying, Cause them that have
charge over the city to draw near, even every
man with his destroying weapon in his hand. 2
And, behold, six men [bosons, particles of light,
fueled of the six noble gases] came from the way
of the higher gate [the mind of strong Gravity],
which lies toward the north [the [hydrogen]
sea]; And every man [has electromagnetism] a
slaughter weapon in his hand.

And [Constance] one man among them was
clothed with linen [integument], with a writer's
ink horn [or writer's case, laptop] by his side:

And they went in, and stood beside the

Michelangelo, Last Judgment (Detail)
1508-1512
The Brazen Altar

brasen altar.

3 And the glory of [Atom Lambda] the God of
Israel was gone up from the cherub [particles:
protons, gluons and neutrons], whereupon he
was, to the threshold of the house [the forebrain].

And he called to the man clothed with linen,
which had the writer's ink horn [laptop case] by
his side; 4 And the LORD said unto him,

Go through the midst of the city, through the
midst of Jerusalem [the brain], and set a mark
upon the foreheads of the men that sigh and that
cry for all the abominations that are done in the
midst thereof.

5 And to the others he said in mine hearing,
Go ye after him through the city, and smite: let
not your eye spare, neither have ye pity: 6 Slay
utterly old and young, both maids, and little
children, and women: but come not near any
man upon whom is the mark; and begin at my
sanctuary [the midbrain]. Then they began at the
ancient men [Z boson, photon and W^3] which
were before the house.

7 And he said unto them, Defile the house
[the e'phods with fecal matter and urine,
contamination, disease], and fill the courts with
the slain: go ye forth. And they went forth, and
slew in [Jerusalem]the city.

8 And it came to pass, while they were slaying
them, and I was left [on my own], that I fell upon
my face, and cried, and said,

Ah Lord GOD! Will thou destroy all the
residue of Israel in thy pouring out of thy fury
upon Jerusalem?

9 Then said he unto me, The iniquity of the
house of Israel and Judah is exceeding* great,
and the land [protons, gluons and neutrons]
is full of [polluted] blood, and the city full of
perverseness:

For they say, The LORD hath forsaken the
earth, and the LORD sees not. 10 And as for me
also, mine eye shall not spare, neither will I have
pity, but I will recompense their way upon their
head.

11 And, behold, the man clothed with linen
[integument, skin, a covering], which had the ink
horn by his side, reported the matter, saying, I
have done as thou hast commanded me.

Ezekiel 9:1-11 KJV

Sandro Botticelli, Birth of Venus

1485–1486

The birth of Venus is the birth of Atom Lambda. Venus is made by strong Gravity. Venus is strong Gravity crystallized. Venus is a homograph for venous, the blood. Having the wings of an eagle, proton holds gluon strong nuclear on his right side. Magnetism, the goose between the legs, lays the golden eggs, gametes. Placed in an electron shell for protection, Atom Lambda is a spirit, the spirit of life. Jealous, as demonstrated by Esau on Jacob, the dragon, electroweak-electromagnetism with the weak interaction, seeks to cover her light, her beauty, her truth.

Revelation 13

The Mark of the Beast

"It is the number of a man; his number is six hundred threescore and six ..."

Period Four, Noble Gas Krypton, Photon

1 And I [John] stood upon the sand [particles, atoms] of the [hydrogen] sea, and [I] saw a beast [photon carrying electromagnetism] rise up out of the sea,

Having seven heads [minds];

And ten horns [voices];

And upon his horns [were] ten crowns [every type of boson and gluons],

And upon his heads [were written] the name of blasphemy [Worship photon; he is god].

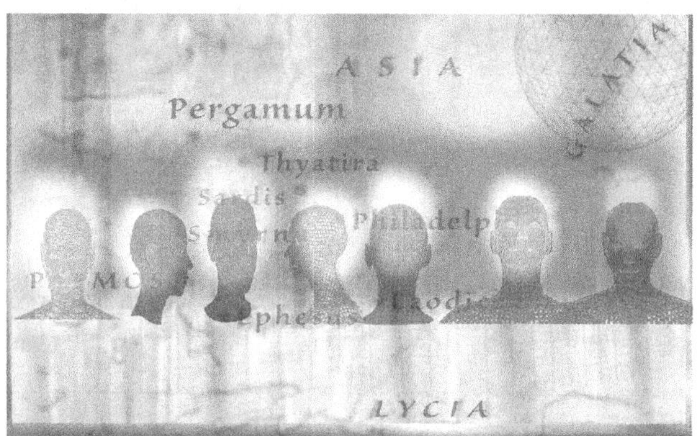

Seven Heads, Minds of the Seven Churches
2012
Smyrna, Pergamos, Thyatira, Ephesus with Sardis, Philadelphia and Laodicea

2 And [photon electromagnetism], the beast which I saw, was like unto a leopard [electroweak force rising up unexpectedly or weak force, bringing calm];

And his feet were as the feet of a bear, [a gluon, a strong attachment, the strong nuclear force; Ourania the right foot and Pandemos the left];

And his mouth as the mouth of a lion [speaking words of wisdom by the gravitational force]:

And the dragon [the unified electroweak-electromagnetism-weak force] gave him [photon] his power [to maim, to destroy], and his seat [in the middle of the forebrain], and great authority [to lead people into the electromagnetic field and to bring reliance upon him and shame upon them].

Electricity Regenerated

3 And I saw one of his heads [electricity], as it were, wounded to death [a single strike];

And [by magnetism], his deadly wound was healed [electricity was brought back to life:

And all the world wondered [asking "Why?"] after the beast [photon electromagnetism].

> 1 Belshazzar the king made a great feast to a thousand of his lords, and drank wine before the thousand. 2 Belshazzar, whiles he tasted the wine, commanded to bring the golden and silver vessels which his father Nebuchadnezzar had taken out of the temple which was in Jerusalem; that the king, and his princes, his wives, and his concubines, might drink therein. 3 Then they brought the golden vessels that were taken out of the temple of the house of God which was at Jerusalem; and the king, and his princes, his wives, and his concubines, drank in them. 4 They drank wine, and praised the gods of gold, and of silver, of brass, of iron, of wood, and of stone. 5 In the same hour came forth fingers of a man's hand, and wrote over against the candlestick upon the plaister of the wall of the king's palace: and the king saw the part of the hand that wrote. 6 Then the king's countenance was changed, and his thoughts troubled him, so that the joints of his loins were loosed, and his knees smote one against another.
>
> Daniel 5:1-6 KJV

Idol Worship

4 And they worshiped the dragon [the unified electroweak-electromagnetism-weak force], which gave power unto the beast [photon]:

And they worshiped the beast [photon, the devil or Satan, death followed by the grave], saying, Who is like unto the beast? Who [constructed with atoms] is able to make war with him?

5 And [by Atom Lambda] there was given unto him a mouth [Cain] speaking great things and blasphemies;

And power was given unto him to continue [in this vein for] forty [four: Judah strong Gravity, Israel strong nuclear, Jerusalem electroweak or Jerusalem weak force];

And two [Ephesus and Sardis] months.[1]

Photon the Blasphemer

6 And he [photon] opened his mouth in blasphemy [lies] against God [Atom Lambda], to blaspheme his [Atom Lambda's] name [Jesus Christ; with photon presenting himself as a god];

And his [Atom's] tabernacle [the brain],

And them [the bosons, gluons] that dwell in heaven [the mind].

7 And it was given unto him [photon] to make war with the saints [protons, gluons and neutrons], and to overcome them:

And power was given [to photon] over all kindreds [through Adam, Eve and Cain (DNA), Abel (RNA)]; and tongues [lights, bosons, gluons, photons]; and nations [the Jewels and the Gentiles.

8 And all that dwell upon the earth shall worship him [photon electromagnetism, the devil and Satan], [including Ephesus and Sardis] whose names are not written in the book of life of the Lamb [Atom Lambda, who was] slain [in the quark-antiquark invasion] from the foundation of the world [before the singularity that is the beginning of all things visible or the *Big Bang*].

Understanding

9 If any man have an ear, let him hear [understand].

10 He that leads [others] into captivity [the electromagnetic field, by introducing debauchery into the thoughts] shall go into captivity:

He that kills with the sword [calling on electromagnetism] must be killed with the sword

1 *Months* is a misnomer meant to keep the mystery secret until it is time.

[electromagnetism].

Here is the patience and the faith of the saints [those tricked and tormented, yet endure].

Cain with Abel

11 And I beheld another beast coming up out of the earth [out of Eve by way of gluon]; and he had two horns like a lamb, and he spake as a dragon [photon].

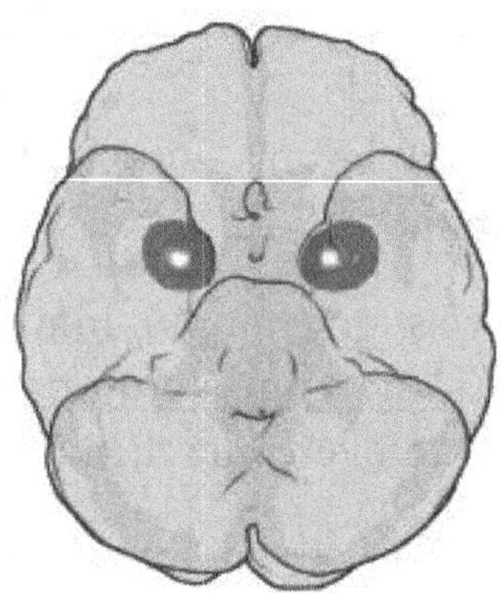

Two Horns, Amygdala

12 And he [the Gentiles] exercises all the power of [photon electromagnetism], the first beast before him; And [he] causes the earth [atoms] and them [particles of mass] which dwell therein [within the nucleus of the atoms that comprise him], to worship the first beast [photon electromagnetism], whose* deadly wound [electricity] was healed [is regenerated by magnetism].

13 And he [the Gentiles] does great wonders, so that he makes fire [electricity stored in a rage] come down from heaven [his mind] on the earth [striking masses, burning flesh, hurling insults] in the sight of men;

The Great Deception

14 And [photon] deceives them that dwell on the earth [Judah, Israel and Jerusalem] by the means of those miracles [pleasure, death, by electricity], which he [the Gentiles] had power to do in the sight of the beast [photon];

Saying to them that dwell on the earth [outside of the nucleus of Atom Lambda: Jerusalem (neutron) and the Gentiles: Ephesus (antiquarks) and Sardis (quarks)]; That they should make an image [an engorgement of the reproductive organs, phallus by hand or mouth] to the beast [photon], which had the wound by a sword [electricity], And did [return to] live.

15 And he [photon] had [the] power to give life [electricity] unto [the phallus] the image of the beast, [causing them to rise up, become engorged]; That [the reproductive organs], the image of the beast should both speak, and cause that as many as *would not* worship the image of the beast [the electrical force in the phallus] should be killed.

Choice, Mark of the Beast

16 And he [electroweak-electromagnetism-weak interaction] causes all, both small and great, rich and poor, free and bond, to receive a mark in [the palm of] their right hand, or in their foreheads [the minds]:

17 And that no man might buy or sell, save he that had the mark [the ability to choose]; or [called upon photon] the name of the beast; or the number of his name.

Understanding

18 Here is wisdom. Let him that has understanding count the number of the beast: For it is the number of [photon electromagnetism], a man;

And his number is Six hundred threescore and six [6-3-6: six quarks; three unified lights as one: Z boson, photon, W^3 boson; and six antiquarks: the zeros are nought]. ✍

Revelation 13:1-18 KJV

All People are Kings

18 O thou king, the most high God [Atom Lambda] gave Nebuchadnezzar [Israel] thy father, a kingdom [e'phod], and majesty [energy], and glory [light], and honour [moral fortitude]:

19 And for the majesty that he gave him, all people [protons, gluons and neutrons], nations [the Jewels or the Gentiles], and languages [life or death], trembled* and feared before him [those]:

Whom he would, he slew*;

And whom he would, he kept alive*;

And whom he would, he set up*;

And whom he would, he put down*.

20 But when his [Nebuchadnezzar's] heart was lifted up, and his mind hardened in pride, he was deposed from his kingly throne, and they took his glory from him:

Blake, Nebuchadnezzar
1805
Nebuchadnezzar (all people), the living dead, existing in the electromagnetic field.

21 And he was driven from the sons of men; and his heart was made like the beasts, and his dwelling was with the wild asses: They fed him with grass like oxen, and his body was wet with the dew of heaven;

Till he knew that the most high God [Atom Lambda] ruled in the kingdom [every energy pod] of men, And that he [Atom Lambda] appoints [to rule] over it [the energy pod] whomsoever he will.

22 And thou, his son, O Belshazzar [Daniel, Jerusalem], hast not humbled thine heart,
though thou knew all this; 23 But [you] have lifted
up thyself against the Lord of heaven; And they [Judah and Israel] have brought the vessels [reproductive organs] of his [Atom Lambda's] house before thee; And you [Z or W^3 boson], and thy lords [photons], thy wives [electricity], and thy concubines [magnetism], have drunk wine [urine] in them;

And thou hast praised the gods [arising from noble gases] of silver, and gold, of brass, iron, wood, and stone, which see not, nor hear, nor know: And [Atom Lambda], the God in whose hand thy breath is, and whose are all thy ways, hast thou not glorified:

24 Then was the part of the hand sent from
him; and this writing was written. 25 And this is the
writing that was written, MENE, MENE, TEKEL,
UPHARSIN. 26 This is the interpretation of the
thing: MENE; God hath numbered thy kingdom,
and finished it. 27 TEKEL; Thou art weighed in
the balances, and art found wanting. 28 PERES;
Thy kingdom is divided, and given to the Medes [electricity] and Persians [magnetism].

Jerusalem Anointed as Third Ruler

29 Then [Atom Lambda] commanded Belshazzar, and they clothed Daniel with scarlet [blood], and put a RNA chain of gold [Z, photon, or W^3 boson] about his neck; and [Atom Lambda] made a proclamation concerning him, that he should be the third ruler [with Atom Lambda first, Israel second and Jerusalem third] in the kingdom [energy pod].

Daniel 5:18-30 KJV

Life on a Shaman's Drum

This is the circle is life. The arrow shoots upward from the singularity, as it is Atom Lambda that made the sun above. The mass above the line are four types of mass: proton, neutron with gluon illustrated as stars. The four lines appearing above the solid line are four forces. The nine lines below are nine muses. The seven holding hands are the seven churches. They stand above the three forces of life. On the left are the conjoined ones, electromagnetism, a quark-antiquark pair. The lines represent the electromagnetic field. The tree is the tree of life. The dots below is waste.

Revelation 14

Messages of Seven Angels

David's Harp, a conduit for healing

And it came to pass, when [photon] the evil spirit from God [Atom Lambda] was upon Saul [the Gentiles, mania and depression], that David [gluon strong nuclear] took an harp, and played with his hand: so Saul was refreshed, and was well, and the evil spirit departed from him.

1 Samuel 16:23 KJV

Atom Lambda: 1 force; 4 in mass and 4 of light

1 And I looked, and, lo, a Lamb [Jesus Christ] stood on the mount Sion [Zion, the forebrain of each person],

And with him [were] an hundred [one, energy] forty [four particles of mass] and four [particles off light] thousand[1], having his Father's name [Atom Lambda] written in their foreheads.

2 And I heard a voice from heaven [Atom Lambda, a proton, hydrogen atom], as the voice of [strong Gravity] many waters [2] [hydrogen waters of the gravitational field and the waste waters of the electromagnetic field],

And as the voice of a great thunder [strong Gravity]: And I heard the voice of harpers [gluons] harping with their harps:

Four beasts defined by physics

3 And they sung, as it were, a new song before the throne, and before the four beasts, all assembled within energy pods, e'phods:

1. Judah, strong Gravity, proton lit by the Higgs boson);
2. Israel, strong nuclear, gluon, self lit;
3. Jerusalem, electroweak-weak, neutron lit by Z or W^3 boson;
4. and the Gentiles, electromagnetism, quark-antiquark taking instructions from Z, photon or W^3 boson],

And the elders [Z boson or the W^3 bosons with photon (electricity) conjoined with photon (magnetism)]:

And no man could learn that song but the hundred [one force] and forty [four, mass] and four [types of light] thousand, which were redeemed from the earth.

First fruits

4 These are they which were not defiled with women [photons]; for they are virgins [having never accepted photon's favors nor entered into the electromagnetic field looking for her pleasure]. These are they which follow [the instructions of] the Lamb [Atom Lambda] wheresoever he goes [leads them]. These were redeemed from among men, being the first fruits unto God [Atom Lambda] and to the Lamb [Jesus Christ].

5 And in their mouth was found no guile: for they are without fault before the throne of God.

1 The zeros are nought.

2 Hydrogen forms: protium, deuterium and tritium

> Hath God cast away his people? God forbid. For I also am an Israelite, of the seed of Abraham, of the tribe of Benjamin. God hath not cast away his people which he foreknew. Wot ye not what the scripture saith of Elias? How he makes intercession to God against Israel, saying, Lord, they have killed thy prophets, and dug down thine altars; and I am left alone, and they seek my life. But what saith the answer of God unto him? I have reserved to myself seven thousand men, who have not bowed the knee to the image of Baal.
>
> Romans 11:1-4 KJV

"... The same shall drink of the wine of the wrath of God ..."

The Announcements

First Angel: Fear Atom Lambda

6 And I saw another angel [Judah, a Higgs boson] fly in the midst of heaven, having the everlasting gospel to preach unto them that dwell on the earth, and to every nation, and kindred, and tongue, and people,

7 Saying with a loud voice, Fear God [Atom Lambda], and give glory to him; for the hour of his judgment is come:

And worship him that made heaven [the mind, the gravitational field], and earth [the e'phods], and the [hydrogen] sea, and the fountains of [waste] waters [the bladder and bowels for elimination in the electromagnetic field].

Second Angel: Fall of Babylon

8 And there followed another angel [Israel, gluon strong nuclear], saying,

Babylon [baby-loins, the reproductive organs] is fallen [is become flaccid], is fallen [the excrement and urine in the reproductive organs released from Babylon], that great city;

Because she [photon] made all nations drink of the wine [urine] of the wrath of her fornication.

Third Angel: Fate

9 And the third angel [Jerusalem Z boson] followed them, saying with a loud voice,

If any man worship [photon] the beast and his image [the reproductive organs],

And receive his mark [through his own choice]
in his forehead [the mind], or in [the palm of] his
hand, 10 The same shall drink of the wine [urine]
of the wrath of God [Atom Lambda], which is
poured out without mixture into the cup of his
indignation;

And he shall be tormented [in the digestive tract] with fire [electricity] and brimstone [magnetism] in the presence of the holy angels [bosons], and in the presence of the Lamb [Atom Lambda]:

11 And the smoke of their torment ascends up for ever and ever:

And they have no rest day nor night, who worship the beast and his image, and whosoever receives the mark of [photon] his name.

Have Patience

12 Here is the patience of the saints: here are they that keep the commandments of God, and the faith of Jesus.

Blessed Assurance

13 And I heard a voice from heaven saying unto me, Write,

Blessed are the dead [Cain, Sardis DNA $C_5H_5N_5$, (without oxygen), carried by the force of electricity], which die in the Lord [having accepted Jesus Christ] from henceforth:

Yea, saith the Spirit, that they may rest from their labours; and their works do follow* them.

14 And I looked, and behold a white [gluon] cloud, and upon the cloud one sat like unto the Son of man, having on his head a golden crown [the sun], and in his hand a sharp sickle [electricity].

Forth Angel Fortune

15 And another angel [Jerusalem W^3 boson] came out of the temple, crying with a loud voice to him [strong nuclear] that sat on the [gluon] cloud,

Thrust in your sickle, and reap: For the time is come for you to reap; for the harvest of the earth is ripe.

16 And [strong nuclear], he that sat on the [gluon] cloud thrust in his sickle on the earth [the e'phods]; and the earth was reaped.

The Conjoined Ones

Fifth Angel: Sardis, electricity

17 And another angel [a photon carrying electricity] came out of the temple which is in heaven, he also having a sharp sickle [electricity].

Sixth Angel: Ephesus, magnetism

18 And another angel [a photon carrying magnetism] came out from the altar [the eyes], which had power over fire [a magnetic field generates an electric field]; and cried with a loud cry to him [gluon] that had the sharp sickle, saying,

Thrust in your sharp sickle, and gather the clusters of the vine of the earth; for her grapes are fully ripe.

19 And the angel thrust in his sickle [electricity] into the earth [the energy pods], and gathered the vine [the vein that transports the blood] of the earth, and cast it into the great winepress [the blood stream] of the wrath of God.

20 And the winepress was trodden without [throughout Jerusalem] the city, and blood came out of the winepress, even unto the horse bridles [3] [the head], by the space [spacetime] of a thousand [one] and six hundred furlongs [six noble gases, chains within DNA and RNA]. [4] ✍

Revelation 14:1-20 KJV

3 A bridle is a device that fits on a horse's head; used for guiding and controlling the horse

4 A furlong is equivalent to 660 feet, 220 yards, 40 rods, or 10 chains.

The Gathering

36 And now therefore thus saith the LORD, the
God of Israel, concerning this city, whereof ye
say, It shall be delivered into the hand of the king
of Babylon by the sword, and by the famine, and
by the pestilence;

37 Behold, I will gather them out of all
countries, whither I have driven them in mine
anger, and in my fury, and in great wrath; and
I will bring them again unto this place, and I will
cause them to dwell safely: 38 And they shall be
my people, and I will be their God:

39 And I will give them one heart, and one
way, that they may fear me for ever, for the good
of them, and of their children after them:

40 And I will make an everlasting covenant
with them, that I will not turn away from them,
to do them good; but I will put my fear in their
hearts, that they shall not depart from me

Jeremiah 32:36-40 KJV

Fear God

Blake, The Lord Answering Job Out of the Whirlwind, Butts set

1803–1805

Revelation 15

Fear Atom Lambda

Tabernacle

A person's head, a portable sanctuary carried by Israelites, Judah, Israel and Jerusalem in the wilderness, the gravitational field. The tent of an augur, for making observations.

Online Etymology Dictionary

1 And I saw another sign in heaven, great and marvellous, seven angels having the seven last plagues; for in them is filled up the wrath of God.

2 And I saw, as it were, a sea of glass [crystallized hydrogen, magnetism][1] mingled with fire [electricity].[2]:

And them that had gotten the victory over the beast, and over his image, and over his mark, and over the number of his name, stand on the sea of glass, having the harps [gluons] of God.

3 And they sing the song of Moses [the Gentiles] the servant of God, and the song of the Lamb [Jesus Christ], saying,

"Great and marvellous are thy works, Lord God Almighty; just and true are thy ways, thou
King of saints. 4 Who shall not fear thee, O Lord,
and glorify thy name?

For thou only art holy: For all nations shall come and worship before thee; for thy judgments are made manifest."

Temple of the Tabernacle of the Testimony

5 And after that I looked, and behold, the temple of the tabernacle of the testimony [the mind] in heaven [the midbrain] was opened:

6 And the seven angels [Ephesus, Smyrna, Pergamos, Thyatira, Sardis, Philadelphia and Laodicea] came out of the temple, having the seven plagues [each plague specific to its source, the six noble gases];

[They were] clothed in pure and white linen [integument, skin, which is the light of the sun];

And having their breasts girded with golden girdles [breast plate covered by muscular tissue].

7 And one of the four beasts gave unto the seven angels seven golden vials full of the wrath of God [Atom Lambda], who lives for ever and ever.

8 And the temple was filled with smoke from the glory [light] of God [Atom Lambda], and from his power [strong Gravity, attractive and repulsive];

And no man [particles of light] was able to enter into the temple [the brain], till the seven plagues of the seven angels were fulfilled. ✍

Revelation 15:1-8 KJV

1 Magnetism is a product of hydrogen, proton; the coupling constant for strong Gravity.

2 Electricity is a consequence of magnetism; coupling constant for gluon strong nuclear.

12 For I will pass through the land of Egypt this night, and will smite all the firstborn [Cain] in the land of Egypt [e-gypt, energy gyp], both man Sardis] and beast [quark]; and against all the gods of Egypt I will execute judgment: I am the LORD. 13 And the blood shall be to you for a token upon the houses [e'phods] where ye are: and when I see the blood, I will pass over you, and the plague shall not be upon you to destroy you, when I smite the land of Egypt.

Exodus 12:12-13 KJV

"Who shall not fear thee, O Lord, and glorify thy name?"

1 And there shall come forth a rod [electricity] out of the stem of Jesse [magnetism]; and a Branch [Jesus Christ] shall grow out of his roots [proton]:

2 And [the Higgs boson], the spirit of the LORD [Atom Lambda], shall rest upon him, [providing] the spirit of wisdom and understanding, the spirit of counsel and might, the spirit of knowledge and of the fear of the LORD;

3 And shall make him of quick understanding in the fear of the LORD: and he shall not judge after the sight of his eyes [what he sees], neither reprove after the hearing of his ears [what he hears]:

4 But with righteousness shall he judge the poor [in spirit, Z bosons], and reprove with equity for [Judah], the meek of the earth:

And he shall smite the earth with [electricity] the rod of his mouth,

And with the breath [noble gas krypton, period four], of his lips shall he slay the wicked [those who choose death over life].

5 And righteousness shall be the girdle of his loins, and faithfulness the girdle of his reins.

6 The wolf [magnetism] also shall dwell with the lamb [proton],

And the leopard [electroweak] shall lie down with the kid [weak]; and the calf [neutron]and the young lion [gluon strong nuclear] and the fatling [quark-antiquark] together;

And a little child [gluon strong nuclear, Israel] shall lead them.

7 And the cow [proton] and the bear [gluon] shall feed; their young ones shall lie down together: and the lion [electromagnetism] shall eat straw like the ox [neutron].

Isaiah 11:1-7 KJV

Death to the First Born, Tenth plague of Egypt

Fürstlich Waldecksche Hofbibliothek Arolsen, Jean Le Pautre

Revelation 16

Last Seven Plagues

A Plague for all people

And this shall be the plague wherewith the LORD will smite all the people that have fought against Jerusalem [the ruler of the brain, body]; Their flesh shall consume away [as necrotic tissue] while they stand upon their feet, and their eyes shall consume away in their holes, and their tongue shall consume away in their mouth.

Zechariah 14:12 KJV

1 And I heard a great voice out of the temple saying to the seven angels, Go your ways, and pour out the vials of the wrath of God upon the earth.

First Angel, Ephesus

2 And [an antiquark] the first went, and poured out his vial upon the earth [the e'phods];

And there fell a noisome [electricity] and grievous sore [magnetism] upon the men which had the mark of the beast [chose photon as their master and ate his food, fecal matter and urine];

And upon them which worshiped his image [the male and female phallus].

Second Angel, Smyrna

3 And the second angel [Smyrna] poured out his vial upon the [hydrogen] sea; and it became as the blood of a dead man: and every living soul [force and light] died in the sea.

Third Angel, Pergamos Ourania

4 And the third angel [gluon] poured out his vial upon the rivers: [proton (Judah), gluon (Israel) and neutron (Jerusalem)]; And [the] fountains of waters: [the antiquark (Ephesus) with quark (Sardis)];

And they became blood [persons that live or die by their choices, their food].

5 And I heard [gluon] the angel of the waters say,

Thou art righteous, O Lord, which art, and wast, and shalt be, because thou hast judged thus.

6 For they have shed the blood of saints [proton and gluon; and prophets [neutrons],

And thou hast given them blood to drink;

For they are worthy [of life by choosing Atom Lambda and of death when following photon, death].

Angel of confirmation, Pandemos

7 And I heard another [gluon Pandemos] out of the altar say, Even so, Lord God Almighty, true and righteous are thy judgments.

Fourth Angel, Thyatira

8 And the fourth angel [Z or W3 boson] poured out his vial upon the sun [separating the Creator from his creation];

And power was given unto him to scorch men with fire [electricity].
9 And men were scorched with great heat [fear, fire in the pit of

Every moving thing that liveth shall be meat for you; even as the green herb have I given you all things.

But flesh with the life thereof, which is the blood thereof, shall ye not eat.

Genesis 9:3-4 KJV

"For they are the spirits of devils, working miracles ..."

the stomach],

And [they] blasphemed [Atom Lambda] the name of God, which hath power over these plagues:

And they repented not [so as] to give him [Atom Lambda] glory.

Fifth Angel, Sardis

10 And the fifth angel [a photon] poured out his vial upon the seat [the reproductive organs] of the beast [of Judah, Israel and Jerusalem and the Gentiles];

And [having no understanding, no light from Atom Lambda] his kingdom [e'phod] was full of darkness;

And [by electromagnetism] they gnawed their
tongues for pain, 11 And blasphemed [Atom
Lambda] the God of heaven because of their pains and their sores,

And [because they had no understanding, they] repented not of their deeds.

Sixth Angel, Philadelphia

12 And the sixth angel poured out his vial upon the great river Euphrates[1];

And the water [from saliva to urine] thereof was dried up, that the way of the kings of the east [gluons] might be prepared.

The Moirai

13 And I saw three unclean spirits, like frogs, come out of the mouth of the dragon [Z, photon, W^3 unified as one],

Blake, Hecate and the Moirai
1795
The three Moirai with the W^3 boson, the spokes person, in the front. With faces hidden are Z boson with long golden hair on the left and photon with the curly hair of magnetism on the right.

1 Euphrates is the transport system for digestion: from the tongue to elimination through the bladder and bowels.

And out of the mouth of the beast: [photon leading Judah, Israel, Jerusalem, and the Gentiles],

And out of the mouth of the false prophet [a Z boson].

14 For they are the spirits of devils [electricity], working miracles [fire erupting in atoms], which go forth unto the kings of the earth [Judah, Israel, Jerusalem, and the Gentiles], and of the whole world [every e'phod], to gather them to the battle of that great day of God Almighty.

Atom Lambda returns

15 Behold, I [Atom Lambda] come as a thief. Blessed is he that watches, and keeps his garments [skin, integument, understanding], lest he walk naked [in ignorance], and they see his shame.

16 And he gathered them together into a place called, in the Hebrew tongue, Armageddon [apocalypses, end of the age].

Seventh Angel, Laodicea

17 And the seventh angel [a gluon] poured out his vial into the air; and there came a great voice out of the temple [the brain] of heaven [the mind], from the throne [the hindbrain], saying, It is done.

The Shaking

18 And there were voices, and thunders, and lightnings;

And there was a great earthquake, such as was not since men were upon the earth, so mighty an earthquake, and so great.

19 And the great city [Jerusalem] was divided into three parts [the forebrain, midbrain and hindbrain];

And the cities [Judah, Israel and Jerusalem, Ephesus with Sardis] of the nations [Jewels and the Gentiles] fell:

And great Babylon [the reproductive system] came in remembrance before God [Atom Lambda], to give unto her the cup of the wine [urine] of the fierceness of his wrath.

20 And every island [quark-antiquark] fled away, and the mountains [electroweak, electromagnetism] were not found.

Plague of Hail

And there fell upon men a great hail out of heaven [crystallization], every stone about the weight of a talent[2]:

And men blasphemed God [Atom Lambda] because of the plague of the hail; for the plague thereof was exceeding great. ✍

Revelation 16:1-21 KJV

2 A talent is a monetary sum believed to consist of, in Attica, 57.75 pounds of silver. Late 13c: refers to "inclination, disposition, will, desire.

Dismantle that Wall of Lies

10 Because, even because they have seduced my people, saying,

Peace; and there was no peace; and one built up a wall, and, lo, others daubed it with untempered mortar: 11 Say unto them which daub it with untempered mortar, that it shall fall: there shall be an overflowing shower; and ye, O great hailstones*, shall fall; and a stormy wind shall rend it.

12 Lo, when the wall is fallen, shall it not be said unto you, Where is the daubing wherewith ye have daubed it? 13 Therefore thus saith the Lord GOD; I will even rend it with a stormy wind in my fury; and there shall be an overflowing shower in mine anger, and great hailstones in my fury to consume it.

14 So will I break down the wall that ye have daubed with untempered mortar, and bring it down to the ground, so that the foundation thereof shall be discovered, and it shall fall, and ye shall be consumed in the midst thereof: and ye shall know that I am the LORD. 15 Thus will I accomplish my wrath upon the wall, and upon them that have daubed it with untempered mortar, and will say unto you,

The wall is no more, neither they that daubed it;

16 To wit, the prophets of Israel which prophesy concerning Jerusalem [the brain], and which see visions of peace for her, and there is no peace, saith the Lord GOD.

Ezekiel 13:10-16 KJV

Blake, Beast and the Whore of Babylon

c 1800

The woman of Babylon with the heart of gold (philanthropy) around her neck, carries a goblet with a poisonous concoction, fecal matter and urine that has been spun into mucus, a reproducing potion for producing offspring. Being over waste management, she sits on "the bottom" of every person.

Revelation 17

Photon, the Great Whore

Blasphemy

The act or offense of speaking sacrilegiously about God or sacred things; profane talk.

Oxford University Press

1 And there came one [a Higgs boson] of the seven angels which had the seven vials, and talked with me, saying unto me,

Come here; I will show unto you the judgment
of [photon] the great whore that sits upon many
[hydrogen] waters [DNA cytosine and thymine,
RNA uracil and the ones grafted in DNA, adenine
conjoined with guanine]: 2 With whom the kings
of the earth [Judah, Israel and Jerusalem, the
Gentiles] have committed fornication, and the
inhabitants of the earth have been made drunk
with the wine [fecal matter and urine, the semen]
of her fornication.

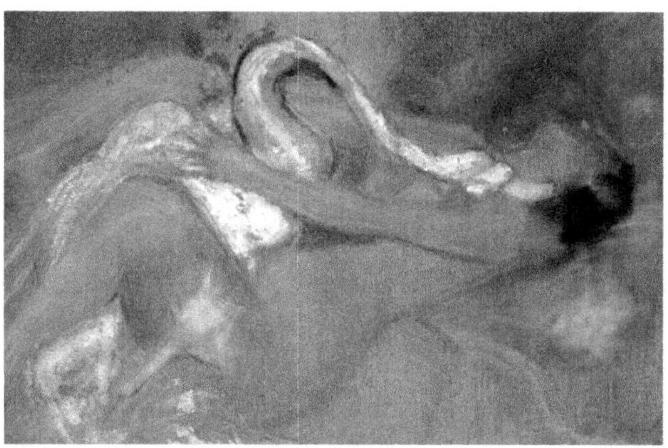

Boldini, Leda with Swan
Unknown date
Leda represents all people. The swan is photon electromagnetism.

3 So he carried me away in the spirit into the wilderness [the electromagnetic field]: and I saw a woman [photon] sit upon a scarlet coloured beast [the gluon octet], full of names of blasphemy; having seven heads [minds of the seven churches] and ten horns [all bosons an particles of light that carry the four universal forces].

4 And the woman [photon electromagnetism] was arrayed in purple [necrotic blood] and scarlet colour [living blood], and decked with gold [lighted neurons] and precious stones [protons ans gluons] and pearls [neutrons], having a golden cup in her hand full of abominations and filthiness of her fornication:

5 And upon her forehead was a name written,

MYSTERY, BABYLON THE GREAT, THE MOTHER OF HARLOTS AND ABOMINATIONS OF THE EARTH.

6 And I saw the woman drunken with the [rotting] blood of the saints [protons and gluons, neutrons], and with the blood of the martyrs of Jesus, [atoms who were crucified within him and died when he died]: And when I saw her, I wondered with great admiration.

7 And the angel said unto me,

Wherefore didst thou marvel? I will tell thee

> Blasphemy: Being filled with all unrighteousness, fornication, wickedness, covetousness, maliciousness; full of envy, murder, debate, deceit, malignity; whisperers, Backbiters, haters of God, spiteful, proud, boasters, inventors of evil things, disobedient to parents, Without understanding, covenant breakers, without natural affection, implacable, unmerciful: Who knowing the judgment of God, that they which commit such things are worthy of death, not only do the same, but have pleasure in them that do them.
>
> Romans 1:29-32 KJV

"I will tell thee the mystery of the woman and the beast that carrieth her ..."

the mystery of the woman, and of the beast that carries her, which has the seven heads and ten horns.

8 The beast that you saw was, and is not; and shall ascend out of the bottomless pit [the bladder and bowels], and go into perdition [the electromagnetic field, the falling]:

Blake, Leviathan
1825
The mouth of Leviathan, of the Levi: electroweak-electromagnetism-weak force, of the electromagnetic field. People are drawn in by choice and systemically destroyed until death.

And they [Sardis and Ephesus, the Gentiles, born from quark-antiquark seeds], that dwell on the earth, shall wonder;

[Those] whose names were not written in the [genetic] book of life from the foundation of the world [the beginning of all things visible, the so-called "big bang"], when they behold the beast [people led by photon] that was* [in the forehead], and is not [there now], and yet is [in the bladder and bowels of all people].

Understanding

9 And here is [to] the mind which has wisdom.

The seven heads are seven mountains [the forebrain], on which the woman [photon] sits*.

10 And there are seven kings [seven churches]:

Five [Ephesus, Smyrna, Pergamos, Thyatira, Sardis] are fallen,

And one [Philadelphia] is [rules now],

And the other [Laodicea] is not yet come; and when he comes, he must continue [to destroy for] a short space.

11 And the beast that was, and is not [gluon Pandemos], even he is the eighth [king], and is of the seven, and goes into perdition.

	Color Charge	By the Noble Gases	Seven (8) Churches
	$(r\bar{b}+b\bar{r})/\sqrt{2}$	helium-Higgs boson for strong-Gravity	Smyrna, male mind
	$(r\bar{r}-b\bar{b})/\sqrt{2}$	neon-argon gluon boson for strong nuclear	Pergamos, male mind
	$(b\bar{g}+g\bar{b})/\sqrt{2}$	xenon-$W\pm$ boson, weak interaction	Thyatira, male mind
The Idols	$-i(b\bar{g}-g\bar{b})/\sqrt{2}$	argon-Z boson, electroweak	Thyatira, female mind
	$-i(r\bar{b}-b\bar{r})/\sqrt{2}$	krypton-photon boson, electromagnetism	Sardis, female mind
	$-i(r\bar{g}-g\bar{r})/\sqrt{2}$	krypton-photon boson, electromagnetism	Ephesus, male mind
	$(r\bar{g}+g\bar{r})/\sqrt{2}$	helium-Higgs boson, strong-Gravity	Philadelphia, female mind
	$(r\bar{r}+b\bar{b}-2g\bar{g})/\sqrt{6}.$	neon-argon gluon boson, strong nuclear	Laodicea, female mind

GLUON'S OCTET OF CHILDREN

NEW GAMETES

12 And the ten horns which you saw are ten kings, [gametes] which have received no kingdom [energy pod, e'phod] as yet; but receive power as kings [after] one hour [one event of insemination] with the beast.

13 These [gametes, new people] have one mind, and shall give their power and strength unto the beast [his parents, within an atom].

14 These [force carrying particles] shall make war with [Atom Lambda] the Lamb; and the Lamb shall overcome them:

For he is Lord of lords [force-carrying particles of light: Higgs, gluon, Z or W^3 boson and photons];

And King of kings [Judah, Israel and Jerusalem, the Gentiles]:

And they that are with him [Atom Lambda]
are [Judah, those] called [into existence], and
[Israel, the] chosen, and [Jerusalem, the] faithful.
15 And he saith unto me,

The waters which you saw, where [photon] the whore sits, are peoples [Judah, Israel and Jerusalem, the Gentiles] and multitudes [particle masses], and nations [Jewels and the Gentiles], and tongues [particles of light].

16 And the ten horns [particles of light] which you saw upon the beast [mankind and the humankind],

These shall hate the whore [photon, where people can exchange life, peace and freedom for a moment of the pleasure of his imaginings],

And shall make her desolate [full of misery] and naked [ignorant],

And shall eat her flesh [fecal matter and urine from the reproductive organs],

And burn her with fire [electricity].

17 For God [Atom Lambda] has put in their hearts to fulfill his will, and to agree*;

And [all] give their kingdom unto the beast, until the words of God shall be fulfilled.

18 And [photon] the woman which you saw is that great city [Babylon], which reigns* over [Judah, Israel and Jerusalem, the Gentiles] the kings of the earth. ✍

Revelation 17:1-18 KJV

Rebuild the Wall

11 So I came to Jerusalem [the forebrain], and
was there three days. 12 And I arose in the night,
I and some few men with me;

Neither told I any man what my God had put
in my heart to do at Jerusalem:

Neither was there any beast with me, save
the beast that I rode upon.

13 And I went out by night by the gate of the
valley, even before the dragon well* [urine], and
to the dung port [bowels], and viewed the walls
of Jerusalem, which were broken down, and the
gates thereof were consumed with fire.

14 Then I went on to the gate of the fountain,
and to the king's pool: but there was no place for
the beast that was under me to pass.

15 Then went I up in the night by the brook, and
viewed the wall, and turned back, and entered
by the gate of the valley, and so returned. 16 And
the rulers knew not where I went, or what I did;
neither had I as yet told it to the Jews, nor to the
priests, nor to the nobles, nor to the rulers, nor
to the rest that did the work.

17 Then said I unto them, Ye see the distress
that we are in, how Jerusalem lies [in] waste, and
the gates thereof are burned with fire:

Come, and let us build up the wall of
Jerusalem, that we be no more a reproach. 18

Then I told them of the hand of my God which
was good upon me; as also the king's words that
he had spoken unto me. And they said, Let us
rise up and build. So they strengthened their
hands for this good work.

Nehemiah 2:11-18 KJV

Forces as Beasts and Dragons

1 And I turned, and lifted up mine eyes, and
looked, and, behold, there came four chariots
out from between two mountains; and the
mountains were mountains of brass. 2 In the
first chariot were red horses; and in the second
chariot black horses; 3 And in the third chariot
white horses; and in the fourth chariot grisled
[electricity] and bay [magnetism] horses.

4 Then I answered and said unto the angel
that talked with me, What are these, my lord?
5 And the angel answered and said unto me,
These are the four spirits [force-carrying light
particles] of the heavens, which go forth from
standing before the Lord of all the earth. 6 The
black horses which are therein go forth into the
north country; and the white go forth after them;
and the grisled [electricity] go forth toward the
south country. 7 And the bay [magnetism] went
forth, and sought to go that they might walk
to and fro through the earth: and he said, Get
you hence, walk to and fro through the earth.
So they walked to and fro through the earth. 8
Then cried he upon me, and spake unto me,
saying, Behold, these that go toward the north
country [the electromagnetic field] have quieted
[Z boson] my spirit in the north country.

Zechariah 6:1-8 KJV

Blake, The Savoy

1896

People trapped in the electromagnetic field with no notion of how to get out.

Revelation 18

Come out of Her, My People

Waxed Rich

Grown rich, become pompous selling pathways to pleasure.

1 And after these things I saw [gluon strong
nuclear] another angel come down from heaven,
having great power; and the earth was lightened
with his glory [the stars]. 2 And he cried mightily
with a strong voice, saying,

Babylon the great is fallen, is fallen, and is become the habitation of devils, and the hold of every foul spirit, and a cage of every unclean and hateful bird.

City of Babylon

Photon is the Idol sitting on her throne, the waste removal, reproductive organs.

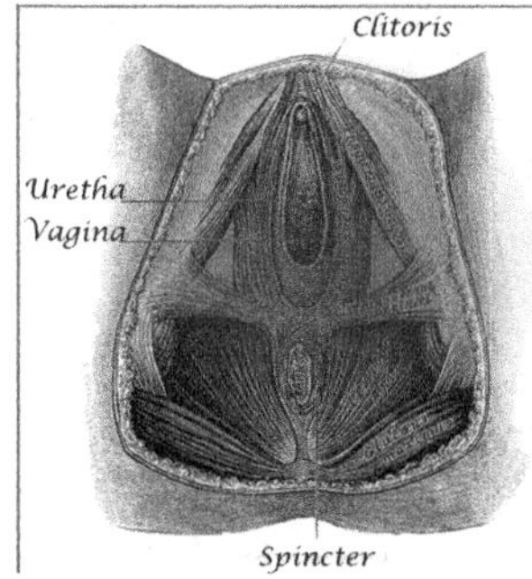

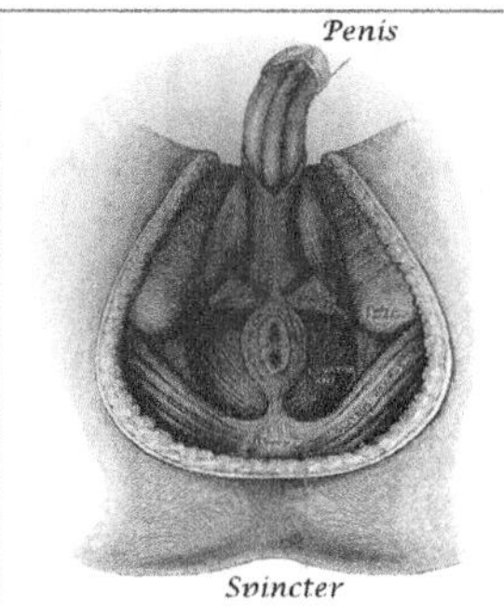

Gray, 408 (female) and 406 (male) perineum
1918

3 For all nations have drunk of the wine [semen spun from fecal matter and urine] of the wrath of her fornication,

And the kings [Judah, Israel and Jerusalem, the Gentiles] of the earth have committed fornication with her,

And the merchants [Z or W^3 boson, photon]
of the earth are waxed rich [with electricity]
through the abundance of her delicacies
[fecal matter and urine, food for quarks and
antiquarks]. 4 And I heard another voice from
heaven, saying,

Come out of her, my people, that you are not partakers of her sins, and that you receive not of her plagues.

5 For her sins [diseased flesh] have reached unto heaven [the forebrain], and [Atom Lambda], God has remembered her iniquities [immoral acts within the e'phods].

6 Reward her [by withdrawing from her] even as she* rewarded you [by taking over your thoughts, your body],

And double unto her double, according to her works [incurable diseases, madness, lewdness]:

In the cup [the bladder and bowels], which she has filled, fill to her double [incurable diseases and madness, by refusing her offer of pleasure].

7 How much she [photon] hath glorified herself, and lived deliciously; So much torment and sorrow give her:

For she says in her heart, I sit a queen, and am no widow, and shall see no sorrow.

> **Merchants:** 1 Now the serpent was more subtil than any beast of the field which the LORD God had made. And he said unto the woman, Yea, hath God said, Ye shall not eat of every tree of the garden? 2 And the woman said unto the serpent, We may eat of the fruit of the trees of the garden: 3 But of the fruit of the tree which is in the midst of the garden, God hath said, Ye shall not eat of it, neither shall ye touch it, lest ye die. 4 And the serpent said unto the woman, Ye shall not surely die: 5 For God doth know that in the day ye eat thereof, then your eyes shall be opened, and ye shall be as gods, knowing good and evil.
>
> Genesis 3:1-5 KJV

"I sit a queen, and am no widow, and shall see no sorrow..."

8 Therefore* shall her plagues come in one day, death, and mourning, and famine; and she shall be utterly burned with fire:

For strong is [Atom Lambda] the Lord God who judges her.

9 And the kings of the earth, who have committed fornication and lived deliciously with her, shall bewail her, and lament for her, when they shall see the smoke of [electricity] her
burning, 10 Standing afar off for the fear of her torment, saying,

Alas, alas, that great city Babylon, that mighty city! For in one hour [one lifetime] is your judgment come.

11 And the merchants [Z or W^3 boson, photon, Jerusalem, Sardis and Ephesus] of the earth shall weep and mourn over her; for no man buys their merchandise any more [exchanging a moment of pleasure for life, even eternal life]:

12 The merchandise of gold [neurons], and silver [antibodies], and precious stones [proton and gluon], and of pearls [neutrons], and fine linen [integument, skin], and purple [blood vessels], and silk [epidermis], and scarlet [oxygenated blood], and all thyine wood [gluons], and all manner vessels of ivory [bones], and all manner vessels of most precious wood [atoms, protons], and of brass [electroweak], and iron [electromagnetism], and marble [weak interaction],

13 And [the strong nuclear interaction, having] cinnamon [sweet and savory], and odours [strong and pleasant or strong and pungent], and ointments [for healing], and frankincense [for speaking the mind without inhibition], and wine [for enjoying], and oil [for understanding], and fine flour [without yeast for baking gametes], and [fields of] wheat [reproduction of mankind],

And beasts [Judah, Israel and Jerusalem, the Gentiles], and sheep [protons], and horses [four universal forces], and chariots [particles of mass: protons, gluons and neutrons], and slaves [quark and antiquarks], and souls of men [bosons of light].

14 And the fruits [fecal matter and urine] that [photon] your soul lusted after, are departed from you, and all things which were dainty and goodly are departed from thee, and you shall find them no more at all.

15 The merchants of these things, which were made rich by her, shall stand afar off for the fear of her torment, weeping and wailing, 16 And
saying,

Alas, alas, that great city, that was clothed in

fine linen [epidermis], and purple [used blood], and scarlet [oxygenated blood], and decked with gold [neurons], and precious stones [protons and gluons], and pearls [neutrons]!

17 For in one hour [lifetime] so great riches is come to nought.

And every shipmaster [atom], and all
the company [of particles] in ships, and
sailors [neutrons], and as many as trade by
[electromagnetic] sea, stood afar off,
18 And
cried when they saw the smoke of her burning,
saying,

What city is like unto this great city!

19 And they cast dust on their heads, and cried, weeping and wailing, saying,

Alas, alas, that great city, wherein were made rich all that had ships in the sea by reason of her costliness! For in one [lifetime] hour is she made desolate.

20 Rejoice over her, you heaven, and you holy apostles [Judah and Israel] and prophets [Jerusalem]; for [Atom Lambda] God has avenged* you on her.

21 And a mighty angel took up a stone like a great millstone, and cast it into the [electromagnetic] sea, saying,

Thus with violence shall that great city Babylon [sitting above the reproduction organs] be thrown down, and shall be found no more at all.

22 And the voice of harpers [gluons], and musicians [neutrons], and of pipers [quarks], and trumpeters [antiquarks], shall be heard no more at all in you;

And no* craftsman [Z boson photon or W^3, like Prometheus (Z boson), who made photon from the waste of the bowels of strong Gravity], his son], of whatsoever craft he is, shall be found any more in you;

And the sound of a millstone [grinding away, grinding fecal matter and urine into oil to satisfy lusts] shall be heard no more at all in you;

23 And the light of a candle [photon] shall shine no more at all in you;

And the voice of the bridegroom and of the bride [voicing their ecstasy on photon's command] shall be heard no more at all in you:

For your merchants were the great men of the earth;

For by thy sorceries [lies, great deceptions] were all nations deceived.

24 And in her [photon electromagnetism] was found the blood of prophets [Jerusalem], and of saints [protons, gluons and neutrons], and of all [mass] that were slain upon the earth [the e'phods]. ✍

Revelation 18:1-24 KJV

He who has ears to hear, let him hear

10 And the disciples came, and said unto
him, Why speak you unto them in parables? 11
He answered and said unto them,Because it
is given unto you to know the mysteries of the
kingdom of heaven, but to them it is not given. 12
For whosoever hath, to him shall be given, and
he shall have more abundance: but whosoever
hath not, from him shall be taken away even that
he hath. 13 Therefore speak I to them in parables:
because they seeing see not; and hearing they
hear not, neither do they understand. 14 And in
them is fulfilled the prophecy of Esaias, which
saith, By hearing ye shall hear, and shall not
understand; and seeing you shall see, and shall
not perceive: 15 For this people's heart is waxed
gross, and their ears are dull of hearing, and
their eyes they have closed; lest at any time they
should see with their eyes, and hear with their
ears, and should understand with their heart,
and should be converted, and I should heal
them. 16 But blessed are your eyes, for they see:
and your ears, for they hear. 17 For verily I say
unto you, That many prophets and righteous
men have desired to see those things which you
see, and have not seen them; and to hear those
things which ye hear, and have not heard them.

Matthew 13:10-17 KJV

Understanding and application

18 Hear ye therefore the parable of the sower.
19 When any one hears the word of the kingdom,
and understands it not, then cometh the wicked
one, and catches away that which was sown
in his heart. This is he which received seed by
the way side. 20 But he that received the seed
into stony places, the same is he that hears the
word, and anon with joy receives it; 21 Yet hath
he not root in himself, but endures for a while: for
when tribulation or persecution arises because
of the word, by and by he is offended. 22 He also
that received seed among the thorns is he that
hears the word; and the care of this world, and
the deceitfulness of riches, choke the word, and
he becomes unfruitful. 23 But he that received
seed into the good ground is he that hears the
word, and understands it; which also bears fruit,
and brings forth, some an hundredfold*, some
sixty*, some thirty.

Matthew 13:18-23 KJV

Slaves grafted in with Jewels

24 Another parable put he forth unto them,
Saying, The kingdom of heaven is likened unto
a man which sowed good seed in his field: 25
But while men slept, his enemy came and sowed
tares among the wheat, and went his way. 26 But
when the blade was sprung up, and brought
forth fruit, then appeared the tares also. 27 So
the servants of the householder came and said
unto him, Sir, didst not thou sow good seed in
thy field? From whence then has it tares? 28 He
said unto them, An enemy hath done this*. The
servants said unto him, Wilt thou then that we
go and gather them up? 29 But he said, Nay; lest
while ye gather up the tares, ye root up also the
wheat with them. 30 Let both grow together until
the harvest: and in the time of harvest I will say
to the reapers, Gather ye together first the tares,
and bind them in bundles to burn them: but
gather the wheat into my barn. And shall cast
them into a furnace of fire: there shall be wailing
and gnashing of teeth.

Matthew 13:24-30 KJV

W^3 boson, a grain of mustard seed

31 Another parable put he forth unto them,
saying,The kingdom of heaven is like to a grain of
mustard seed, which a man took, and sowed in
his field: 32 Which indeed is the least of all seeds:
but when it is grown, it is the greatest among
herbs, and becomes a tree, so that the birds of
the air come and lodge in the branches thereof.

Matthew 13:31-32 KJV

Michelangelo, Creation of Adam

1511

Wedding of the Lambda, Adam and Atom Lambda, the purveyor of life in the hindbrain, the rhombencephalon.

Revelation 19

Marriage of the Lambda

Fornication

The commitment to fight against Atom Lambda, against life. Fornication with photon means Judah and Israel, Jerusalem succumbs to eating fecal matter and urine, the food of the quark-antiquark pairs, the Gentiles, who are slaves to their instincts. By photon, the Jewels eat all manner of toxicity, which serves to kill the people, protons, gluons and neutrons, which comprise us.

Highest Praise for Atom Lambda

1 And after these things I heard a great voice of much people [singing in unison: forces, light particles and particles of mass] in heaven [the brain], saying,

Alleluia; Salvation, and glory, and honour, and power, unto [Atom Lambda] the Lord our God:

2 For true and righteous are his judgments:
for he has judged [photon electromagnetism] the
great whore, which did corrupt the earth [energy
pods] with her fornication, and has avenged the
blood of his servants at her hand. 3 And again
they said, Alleluia. And her smoke [of electricity
burning] rose up for ever and ever.

4 And the four [Z boson or W^1 or W^2 or W^3 boson] and twenty [two] elders [photon carrying electricity conjoined with photon carrying magnetism]; and the four beasts [Judah, Israel and Jerusalem, the Gentiles] fell down and worshiped God [Atom Lambda strong Gravity] that sat on the throne [in the hindbrain], saying, Amen [He is all men]; Alleluia.

5 And a voice [Gabriel, Z or W^3 boson] came out of the throne, saying,

Praise our God, all you, his servants [protons, gluons and neutrons], and you [quarks and antiquarks] that fear him, both small and great.

Marriage of the Lambda

6 And I heard, as it were, the voice of a great multitude [Israel, gluons, strong nuclear], and as the voice of many waters [Jerusalem, neutrons, electroweak-weak], and as the voice of mighty thunderings [Judah, protons, strong Gravity], saying,

Alleluia: for [Atom Lambda] the Lord God
omnipotent reigns. 7 Let us be glad and rejoice,
and give honour to him:

For the marriage of the Lamb [the creation holding on to his Creator] is come, and his wife [a boson of light] has made herself ready.

8 And to her was granted that she should be
arrayed in fine linen [the light of the sun], clean
and white: for the fine linen is the righteousness
of saints [mass and light particles, atoms]. 9 And
he saith unto me, Write,

Be you also ready

Blessed are they which are called [like the ten virgins] unto the marriage supper of the Lamb. And he said unto me,

These are the true sayings of God.

10 And I [John] fell at his feet to worship him

Marriage of the Lambda

24 Therefore shall a man leave [the womb] his father and his mother, and shall cleave unto his wife [the Lambda of his singularity, Atom]: and they shall be one flesh [energy pod and mind together as one]. 25 And [being newly pushed from his mother's womb], they were both naked, the man and his wife, and were not ashamed.

Genesis 2:24-25 KJV

"For the marriage of the Lamb is come ..."

[Jesus Christ]. And he said unto me,

See [that] you do it not: I am your fellow servant, and of your brethren that have the testimony of Jesus:

Worship God [Atom Lambda]: For the testimony of Jesus is the spirit of prophecy.

11 And I saw heaven opened, and behold a white horse [strong Gravity]; and he that sat upon him was called Faithful and True: And in righteousness [gravitas], he does judge and make war.

12 His eyes [the Higgs boson, Z or W^3 boson] were as a flame of fire, and on his head were many crowns [even some seven billion crowns]; and he had a name written, that no man knew, but he himself [deoxyribonucleic acid].

13 And he was clothed with a vesture [integument] dipped in blood:

And his name is called [Atom Lambda] The Word of God.

14 And the [immunological and biological] armies which were in heaven followed him upon white horses [gravity, strong nuclear], clothed in fine linen [light of the sun], white and clean.

15 And out of his mouth goes a sharp sword [Z boson, electricity], that with it he should smite the nations:

And he shall rule them with a rod of iron [Z or W^3 boson]:

And he [Z or W^3 boson] treads the winepress [in the blood that gives life and ends life by spreading disease, misery], of the fierceness and wrath of Almighty God [Atom Lambda].

16 And he has on his vesture [brain] and on his thigh [reproductive organ] a name written,

KING OF KINGS [Judah, Israel and Jerusalem, the Gentiles and all of the living that is within them], AND LORD OF LORDS [particles of light].

The Feast

17 And I saw an angel [Z or W^3 boson] standing in the sun; and he cried with a loud voice, saying to all the fowls [photons] that fly in the midst of heaven,

Come and gather yourselves together unto
the supper of the great God; 18 That you may eat
the flesh of kings [all born with crowns], and the flesh of captains [Judah], and the flesh of mighty men [Israel], and the flesh of horses [forces];

And [the particles of mass] of them that sit on them;

And the flesh of all men, both free [Judah,

What? Know ye not that your body [mind] is the temple of [Atom Lambda], the Holy Ghost, which is in you [in the hindbrain], which ye have [because] of God, and ye are not your own? For ye are bought with a price [an infinite number of atoms, particles of mass destroying, replenishing, replacing; with light fed by the sun, Atom Lambda]: therefore glorify God in your body [e'phod], and in your spirit [boson or gluon light], which are God's.

1 Corinthians 6:19-20 KJV

Israel and Jerusalem] and bond [Ephesus and Sardis], both small and great.

19 And I saw the beast [photon electromagnetism leading Jewels and the Gentiles, and the energy, mass and light that comprise them],

And the kings of the earth [Judah, Israel and Jerusalem, the Gentiles], and their [brooding biological] armies, gathered together to make war against him [Atom Lambda] that sat on the horse [strong Gravity], and against his army [of gluons].

20 And [photon electromagnetism] the beast was taken [out of the minds of the Jewels], and with him, the false prophet [Z or W^3 boson] that wrought miracles [lies] before him, with which he deceived them that had received the mark of the beast [and chose to follow photon in the electromagnetic field of death], and them that worshiped his [photon's] image [the phallus, on hands and knees].

These both [Z boson and photon] were cast alive into a lake of fire [the sun] burning with brimstone [magnetism].

21 And the remnant [light particles that are from the beginning] were slain with [gluon strong nuclear] the sword of him that sat upon the [white] horse [strong Gravity], which sword proceeded out of his mouth:

And all the fowls [photons, quark-antiquark pairs] were filled with their [rotting, necrotic] flesh. ✍

Revelation 19:1-21 KJV

LORD God Omnipotent

2 Dominion and fear are with him, he makes peace in his high Places [the
brain]. 3 Is there any number of his armies? And upon whom doth not his
light arise? 4 How then can man be justified with God? Or how can he be
clean that is born of a woman? 5 Behold even to the moon, and it shines not;
yea, the stars are not pure in his sight. 6 How much less [is] man, that is a
worm [a force-carrying particle]? And the son of man [Cain, the Gentiles],
which is a worm [a two-headed beast] ?

Job 25:2-6 KJV

The Word of God

1 In the beginning was the Word [Atom Lambda], And the Word [Atom Lambda] was with God [strong Gravity],

And the Word [Atom Lambda] was God [strong Gravity].

2 The same was in the beginning [period one, proton, hydrogen][1] with God [strong Gravity].

3 All things were made by him [Atom Lambda] and without him was not any thing made that was made.

4 In him [strong Gravity] was life;

And the life was the light [understanding] of men.

5 And [Atom Lambda] the light shines in darkness [the electromagnetic field, ignorance]; and the darkness [the electromagnetic field] comprehended it not.

John 1:1-12 KJV

1 Hydrogen, as atomic H, is the most abundant chemical element in the universe, making up 75 percent of normal matter by mass and more than 90 percent by number of atoms. Hydrogen: From Wikipedia, the free encyclopedia

Behold, the bridegroom comes

1 Then shall the kingdom of heaven be likened
unto ten virgins, which took their lamps, and
went forth to meet the bridegroom. 2 And five
of them were wise, and five were foolish. 3 They
that were foolish took their* lamps, and took
no oil [knowledge, understanding and wisdom]
with them: 4 But the wise took oil [knowledge,
understanding and wisdom] in their vessels with
their lamps. 5 While the bridegroom tarried, they
all slumbered and slept.

6 And at midnight there was a cry made,
Behold, the bridegroom comes; go you out to
meet him. 7 Then all those virgins arose, and
trimmed their lamps. 8 And the foolish said unto
the wise, Give us of your oil; for our lamps are
gone out. 9 But the wise answered, saying, Not
so; lest there be not enough for us and you: but
go you rather to [Z, photon or W[3]] them that sell,
and buy for yourselves.

10 And while they went to buy, [Atom Lambda]
the bridegroom came; and they that were ready
went in with him to the marriage: and the door
was shut. 11 Afterward* came also the other
virgins, saying, Lord, Lord, open to us. 12 But he
answered and said, Verily I say unto you, I know
you not.

Matthew 25:1-12 KJV

Michelangelo, Last Judgment

1508-1512

Book of Life written by strong Gravity records the physics of life, the energy, mass and light present in the conception of the six noble gases. The large book of life is a record of day to day genetic records, what was ingested, digested, eliminated in the chain, written from the foundation of the world.

Revelation 20

Atom Lambda, Purveyor of Life

1000 Years

But, beloved, be not ignorant of this one thing, that one day is with the Lord [in spacetime is] as a thousand years, and a thousand years as one day.

2 Peter 3:8 KJV

1 And I saw an angel [gluon strong nuclear]
come down from heaven, having the key [to the
mouth] of the bottomless pit [the bladder and
bowels]; and a great [genetic] chain in his hand.
2 And he laid hold on the dragon [photon], that
old serpent, which is the Devil [electricity], and
Satan [magnetism], and bound him [in a genetic
chain, RNA polymerase, a form of nucleotidyl
transferase for] a thousand years [one day];

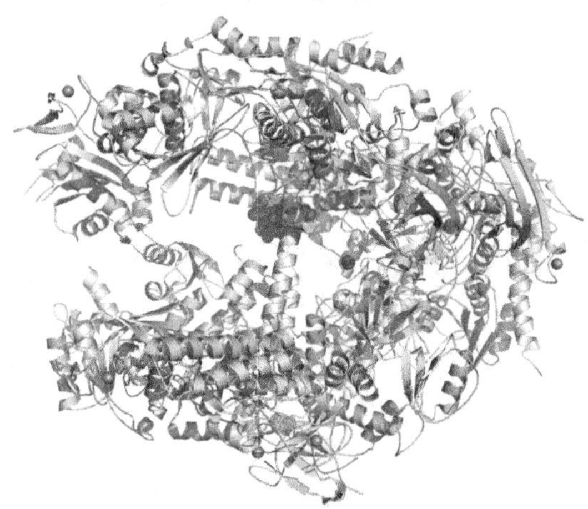

Alpha-Amanitin RNA polymerase II complex 1K83
2007
Ribbon diagram of Saccharomyces cerevisiae RNA polymerase II in complex with amanitin. Active site magnesium ion visible near center.

3 And [the angel] cast him [photon] into the
bottomless pit [the bladder and bowels], and shut
him up, and set a [biohazard] seal upon him,
that he should deceive the nations no more, till
the thousand years [one day] should be fulfilled:

And after that he [photon] must be loosed a little season.

The First Resurrection

4 And I saw thrones [in the forebrain, midbrain
and hindbrain], and they sat upon them, and
judgment was given unto them:

And I saw the souls [lights] of them that were beheaded for the witness of Jesus, and for [Atom Lambda] the word of God [strong Gravity];

Aurora Consurgens
15th Century
Photon the serpent with those he has beheaded; their light, the accumulated knowledge, understanding and wisdom, usurped for a moment of pleasure.

The molecular basis for genes is (DNA) deoxyribonucleic acid. DNA is composed of a chain of nucleotides, of which there are four types: adenine (Sardis, A), cytosine (Judah, C), guanine (Ephesus, G), and thymine (Israel, T) and RNA uracil (Jerusalem, A, G, C and U.). Genetic information exists in the sequence of these nucleotides, and genes exist as stretches of sequence along the DNA chain. Viruses are the only exception to this rule—sometimes viruses use the very similar molecule RNA instead of DNA as their genetic material. Viruses cannot reproduce without a host and are unaffected by many genetic processes, so tend not to be considered living organisms.

"Blessed and holy is he that hath part in the first resurrection ..."

And which had not worshiped the beast [photon leading Judah, Israel and Jerusalem, the Gentiles], neither his [phallic] image*, neither had received his mark [choice] upon their foreheads [in their minds], or in [the palm of] their hands;

And they [the ones that have been beheaded] lived and reigned with Christ a thousand years, [spacetime].

5 But the rest of the dead lived not again until the thousand years were finished. This is the first resurrection.

6 Blessed and holy is he that has part in the first resurrection [from the electromagnetic field]:

Blake, Overthrow of Apollo, gluon Pandemos
Ca. 1809
Electromagnetism expelled from gluon, Z boson or W3 imprisoned, the fearful hide their faces.

On such, the second death has no power;

But they shall be priests [people with minds, lights to think, listen] of God [strong Gravity] and of Christ [Atom Lambda], And shall reign with him a thousand years.

Myles, Eve, base illustration
1993
Compilation of good and evil (Connie Allen).

The Devil, Satan loosed

7 And when the thousand years are expired, Satan shall be loosed out of his prison [the genetic chain];

8 And shall go out to deceive the nations [Jewels and the Gentiles], which are in the four quarters of the earth [of Judah, Israel and Jerusalem, Sardis conjoined with Ephesus

in], Gog [electricity] and Magog [magnetism; components of the electromagnetic field];

To gather them together to battle [life against death, protons, gluons and neutrons against quark-antiquarks, bacterial bodies], the number of whom is as the sand of the sea.

9 And they went up on the breadth of the earth [up the middle of the back, climbing up the spine, from the bowels], and encompassed the camp of the saints about, and [Jerusalem] the beloved city: And fire came down from [Atom Lambda] God out of heaven [the sun], and devoured them.

10 And the devil [electricity] that deceived them [into eating fecal matter and urine] was cast into the lake of fire [the sun] and brimstone [magnetism],

Where the beast [photon ruling over Judah, Israel and Jerusalem, the Gentiles], and the false prophet [Z or W^3 boson] are, and [he] shall be tormented day and night for ever and ever.

11 And I saw a great white throne [the sun], and him [Atom Lambda] that sat on it, from whose face the earth and the heaven fled away; and there was found no place for them.

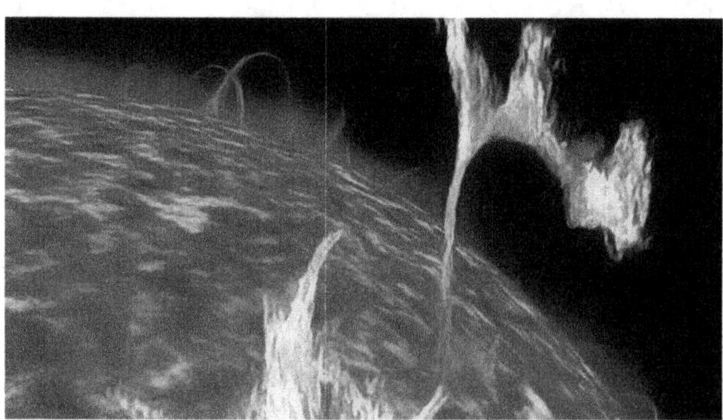

The Sun
2012
Solar Flares.

Genetic Evidence

12 And I saw the dead [Sardis conjoined with Ephesus], small [quarks] and great [antiquarks], stand before God;

And the [physics] books were opened:

And another book was opened, which is the [genetic] book of life:

And the dead [quark-antiquark pairs, Sardis the Gentiles] were judged out of those things which were written in the books, according to their works.

13 And the [electromagnetic] sea gave up the dead which were in it;

And death [electricity] and hell [on earth, magnetism] delivered up the dead [quarks with antiquarks, electricity], which were in them:

And they [Judah, Israel and Jerusalem, Ephesus] were judged, every man, according to their works [the innate behaviours and acquired behaviours, choices, as recorded in the genetic code, the DNA chain, which is the book of life].

14 And death [electricity] and hell [magnetism] were cast into the lake of fire [the sun].

This is the second death. 15 And whosoever [Sardis conjoined with Ephesus] was not found written in the book of life was cast into the lake of fire. ✍

Revelation 20:1-15 KJV

Magnetism, leaven

33 Another parable spake he unto them; The
kingdom of heaven is like unto leaven, which a
woman took, and hid in three measures of meal,
till the whole was leavened. 34 All these things
spake Jesus unto the multitude in parables;
and without a parable spake he not unto them:
35 That it might be fulfilled which was spoken
by the prophet, saying, I will open my mouth in
parables; I will utter things which have been kept
secret from the foundation of the world.

Matthew 13:33-35 KJV

End of the world as we know it

36 Then Jesus sent the multitude away, and
went into the house: and his disciples came unto
him, saying, Declare unto us the parable of the
tares of the field. 37 He answered and said unto
them, He that sows the good seed is the Son of
man; 38 The field is the world*; the good seed are*
the children of the kingdom; but the tares are the
children of the wicked one; 39 The enemy that
sowed them is the devil*; the harvest is the end
of the world; and the reapers are the angels. 40
As therefore the tares are gathered and burned
in the fire; so shall it be in the end of this world.
41 The Son of man shall send forth his angels,
and they shall gather out of his kingdom all
things that offend, and them which do iniquity;
42 And shall cast them into a furnace of fire: there
shall be wailing and gnashing of teeth. 43 Then
shall the righteous shine forth as the sun in the
kingdom of their Father. Who hath ears to hear,
let him hear.

Matthew 13:36-43 KJV

The Net

47 Again, the kingdom of heaven is like unto a
net, that was cast into the sea, and gathered of
every kind: 48 Which, when it was full, they drew
to shore, and sat down, and gathered the good
into vessels, but cast the bad away. 49 So shall it
be at the end of the world: the angels shall come
forth, and sever the wicked from among the just,
50 And shall cast them into the furnace of fire:
there shall be wailing and gnashing of teeth.

51 Jesus saith unto them, Have you understood
all these things? They say unto him, Yea, Lord.

Matthew 13:47-51 KJV

Scribes, changers of DNA code

52 Then said he unto them, Therefore* every
scribe [living person contributing to changes
in Atom Lambda's genetic code], which is
instructed unto the kingdom of heaven [the
mind], is like unto a man that is a householder,
which brings forth out of his treasure things new
and old.

Matthew 13: 6:52 KJV

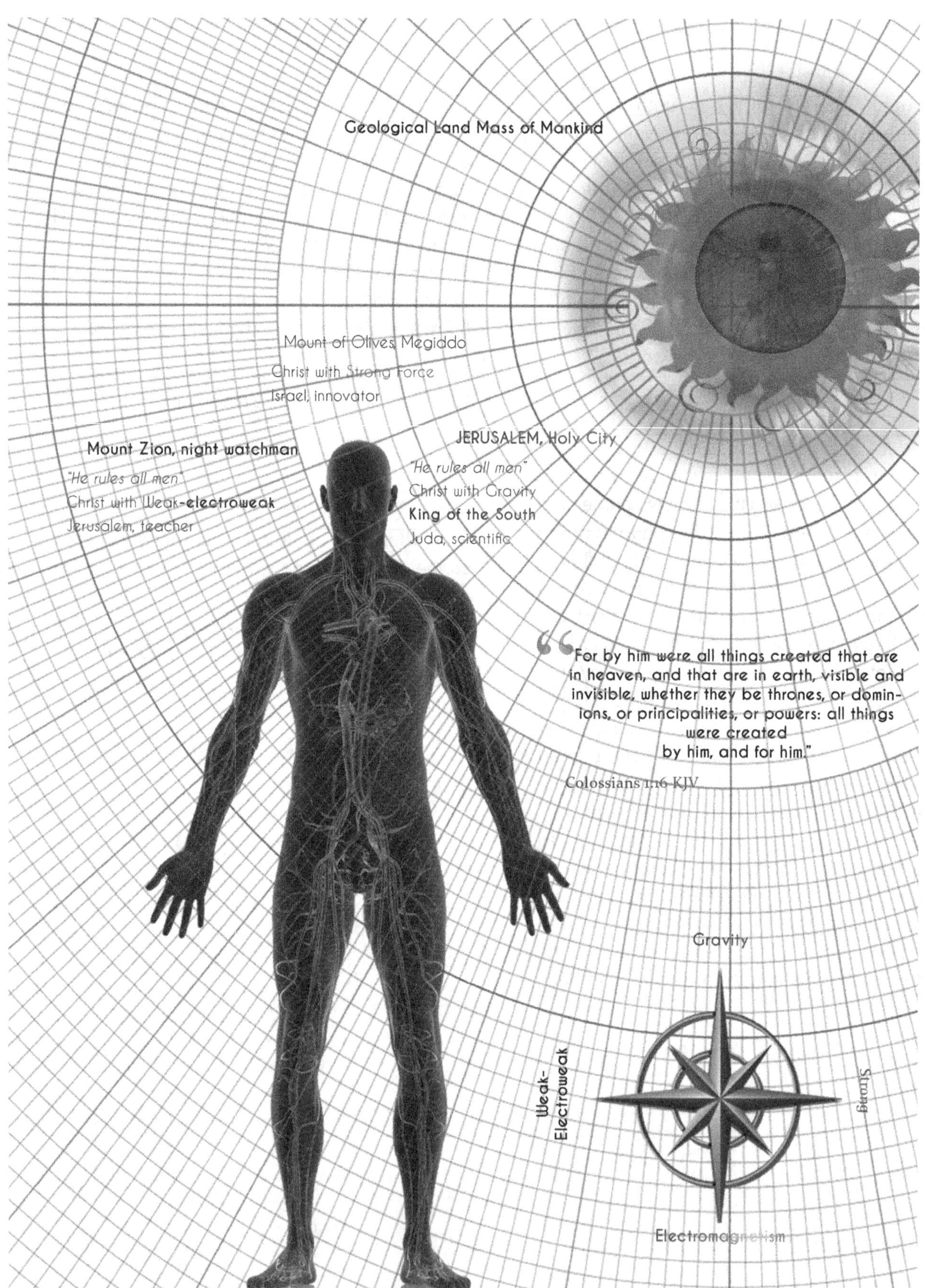
Geological Land Mass of Mankind
Mount of Olives, Megiddo
Christ with Strong Force
Israel, innovator
Mount Zion, night watchman
"He rules all men"
Christ with Weak-electroweak
Jerusalem, teacher
JERUSALEM, Holy City
"He rules all men"
Christ with Gravity
King of the South
Juda, scientific
"For by him were all things created that are in heaven, and that are in earth, visible and invisible, whether they be thrones, or dominions, or principalities, or powers: all things were created by him, and for him."
Colossians 1:16 KJV
Gravity
Weak-Electroweak
Strong
Electromagnetism

Revelation 21

Rebuild Jerusalem

> 24 Thus says the LORD, your redeemer, and he that formed
> you from the womb, I am the LORD that makes all things; that
> stretches forth the heavens alone; that spread abroad the earth
> by myself; 25 That frustrates the tokens of the liars, and makes
> diviners mad; that turns wise men backward, and makes their
> knowledge foolish; 26 That confirms the word of his servant,
> and performs the counsel of his messengers; that saith to
> Jerusalem, You shalt be inhabited; and to the cities of Judah,
> Ye shall be built, and I will raise up the decayed places thereof:
> 27 That saith to the deep, Be dry, and I will dry up thy rivers.
>
> Isaiah 44:24-27 KJV

1 And I saw a new heaven [mind] and a new earth [energy pod]: for the first heaven and the first earth were passed away; and there was no more [electromagnetic] sea [perdition, in the midst if the hydrogen ocean].

The Holy City

2 And I John saw the holy city, new Jerusalem, coming down from God [strong Gravity] out of heaven [Atom Lambda], prepared as a bride adorned [with Jewels] for her husband.

3 And I heard a great voice out of heaven saying, Behold, the [sanctuary] tabernacle of [Atom Lambda], God is with men [people], and he will dwell with them [in the hindbrain, just above the central nervous system];

And they [Judah, Israel and Jerusalem, Ephesus] shall be his people;

And God himself [Atom Lambda strong Gravity] shall be with them, and be their God.

4 And God [Atom Lambda] shall wipe away all tears from their eyes;

And there shall be no more death [from electricity], neither sorrow, nor crying [magnetism], neither shall there be any more pain [electroweak-weak force]: for the former things [photons] are passed away.

The Second Death

5 And [Atom Lambda] he that sat upon the throne said,

Behold, I make all things new. And he said
unto me, Write: for these words are true and
faithful. 6 And he said unto me,

It is done. I am Alpha and Omega, the
beginning and the end. I will give unto him that
is athirst of the fountain of the [hydrogen] water
of life freely. 7 He that overcomes shall inherit
all things; and I will be his God, and he shall be
my son.

8 But the fearful, and unbelieving, and the abominable, and murderers, and whoremongers, and sorcerers, and idolaters, and all liars, shall have their part in the lake which burns with fire [electricity] and brimstone [magnetism]: which is the second death.

Last Seven Plagues

9 And there came unto me [Laodicea] one of the seven angels which had the seven vials full of the seven last plagues, and [she] talked with me, saying,

Come hither, I will shew you the bride, the Lamb's wife.

10 And he carried me away in the spirit to

CYRUS, THE SHEPHERD

28 That saith of Cyrus, He is my shepherd, and shall perform all my pleasure: even saying to Jerusalem, Thou shalt be built; and to the temple, Thy foundation shall be laid.

Isaiah 44: 28 KJV

"... The city had no need of the sun, neither of the moon, to shine in it ..."

a great and high mountain [the sun], and shewed me that great city, the holy Jerusalem, descending out of heaven [Atom Lambda] from God, 11 Having the glory [light] of God:

And her light was like unto [a proton], a stone most precious, even like a jasper stone [a gluon], clear as crystal;

12 And had a wall, great and high [separating living mass from the elements of death, all wastes, blood, urine and excrement];

THE STANDARD MODEL OF PARTICLE PHYSICS

THE GATES

GATES
1993
Sun of man

And [Jerusalem the city] had twelve gates [entry and exit points], and at the gates twelve angels, and names written thereon, which are the names of the twelve tribes of the children of Israel:

13 On the east [gluon strong nuclear, there are] three gates [two eyes, one nose and one mouth];

On the north [an antiquark, magnetism, there are] three gates [two eyes, one nose and one mouth];

On the south [proton strong gravity, there are] three gates [two eyes, one nose and one mouth];

And on the west [neutron weak interaction, there are] three gates [two eyes, one nose and one mouth].

Twelve Apostles of Atom Lambda

Gravity	strong nuclear	electroweak	weak
Proton	gluon	neutron	antiquark
Higgs	gluon	W^3	U(1)em
Judah	Israel	Jerusalem	Ephesus

And in them [the twelve foundations are] the

names of the twelve apostles of the Lamb [Atom Lambda].

Measurements

15 And he that talked with me had a golden reed [W^3 weak force] to measure [Jerusalem] the city, and the gates [entry points] thereof, and the wall [of atoms] thereof.

16 And the city lies foursquare [as the four universal forces], and the length* [mass] is as large as the breadth [light]: and he measured the city with the reed* [weak force], twelve [12] thousand furlongs [legs]. The length and the breadth [mass] and the height [light] of it are equal.

17 And he measured the wall thereof, an hundred [One God]; and forty [four forces], and four [people: Judah, Israel and Jerusalem, Ephesus, the visible of the four forces]; cubits [is a misnomer], according to the measure of a man, that is, of the angel.

Precious Stones

18 And the building of the wall of it was of
jasper [atoms, protons]: and the city was pure
gold [neurons], like unto clear glass. 19 And
the foundations of the wall of the city were
garnished with all manner of precious stones
[particles].

The first foundation was jasper [proton]; the second, sapphire [gluon]; the third, a chalcedony [neutron]; the fourth, an emerald [antiquark];

20 The fifth, sardonyx [Judah]; the sixth, sardius [Israel]; the seventh, chrysolite [Jerusalem]; the eighth, beryl [Ephesus];

The ninth, a topaz [Higgs boson]; the tenth, a chrysoprasus [gluon]; the eleventh, a jacinth [W^3 bosom]; the twelfth, an amethyst [U(1)em].

Pearls

21 And the twelve gates were twelve pearls [minds holding knowledge, understanding and wisdom]; every* several gate [eyes, nose and mouth] was of one pearl:

And the street of the city was pure gold, as it were, transparent glass [invisible to the naked eye].

22 And I saw no temple [for kneeling, praying] therein*: for the Lord God Almighty [Atom Lambda] and [Jesus Christ] the Lamb are the temple of it [and every thought may be considered as prayer].

Enlightened

23 And the city had no need of the [morning] sun, neither of the [night] moon, to shine in it:

For the glory of God [Atom Lambda] did
lighten it, and the Lamb is the light thereof. 24
And the nations of them which are saved [the
Jewels and the Gentiles] shall walk in the light
of it: and the kings of the earth do bring their
glory [bosons] and honour [righteousness] into
it. 25 And the gates [eyes, nose and mouth] of it
shall not be shut at all by day: for there shall be
no night there.

26 And they shall bring the glory and honour
of the nations into it. 27 And there shall in no
wise enter into it any thing that defiles, neither
whatsoever works abomination, or makes a lie:
but they [Judah, Israel and Jerusalem] which are
written in the Lamb's book of life [the standard
model of particle physics]. ✍

Revelation 21:1-27 KJV

Return to Atom Lambda

1 Yet now hear, O Jacob my servant; and Israel, whom I have chosen: 2 Thus saith the LORD that made you, and formed you from the womb, which will help you; Fear not, O Jacob, my servant; and you, Jesurun [Judah], whom I have chosen. 3 For I will pour water upon him that is thirsty, and floods upon the dry ground: I will pour my spirit upon your seed [offspring], and my blessing upon thine offspring: 4 And they shall spring up as among the grass, as willows by the water courses. 5 One shall say, I am the LORD'S; and another shall call himself by the name of Jacob; and another shall subscribe with his hand unto the LORD, and surname himself by the name of Israel. 6 Thus saith the LORD the King of Israel, and his redeemer the LORD of hosts; I am the first, and I am the last; and beside me there is no God. 7 And who, as I, shall call, and shall declare it, and set it in order for me, since I appointed the ancient people? And the things that are coming, and shall come, let them shew unto them. 8 Fear ye not, neither be afraid: have not I told thee from that time, and have declared it? You are even my witnesses. Is there a God beside me? Yea, there is no God; I know not any. 9 They that make a graven image are all of them vanity; and their delectable things shall not profit; and they are their own witnesses; they see not, nor know; that they may be ashamed. 10 Who has formed a god, or molten a graven image that is profitable for nothing? 11 Behold, all his fellows shall be ashamed: and the workmen, they are of men: let them all be gathered together, let them stand up; yet they shall fear, and they shall be ashamed together.

12 The smith with the tongs both works in the coals, and fashions it with hammers, and works it with the strength of his arms: yea, he is hungry, and his strength fails: he drinks no water, and is faint. 13 The carpenter stretches out his rule; he marks it out with a line; he fits it with planes, and he marks it out with the compass, and makes it after the figure of a man, according to the beauty of a man; that it may remain in the house. 14 He hews him down cedars, and taketh the cypress and the oak, which he strengthens for himself among the trees of the forest: he plants an ash, and the rain doth nourish it. 15 Then shall it be for a man to burn: for he will take thereof, and warm himself; yea, he kindles it, and bakes bread; yea, he makes a god, and worships it; he makes it a graven image, and falls down thereto. 16 He burns part thereof in the fire; with part thereof he eats flesh; he roasts roast, and is satisfied: yea, he warms himself, and saith, Aha, I am warm, I have seen the fire: 17 And the residue thereof he makes a god, even his graven image: he falls down unto it, and worships it, and prays unto it, and saith, Deliver me; for thou art my god.

18 They have not known nor understood: for he [Atom Lambda] has shut their eyes, that they cannot see; and their hearts, that they cannot understand. 19 And none considers in his heart, neither is there knowledge nor understanding to say, I have burned part of it in the fire; yea, also I have baked bread upon the coals thereof; I have roasted flesh, and eaten it: and shall I make the residue thereof an abomination? Shall I fall down to the stock of a tree? 20 He feeds on ashes [food consumed with electricity, fecal matter and urine]: a deceived heart hath turned him aside, that he cannot deliver his soul, nor say, Is there not a lie in my right hand? 21 Remember these, O Jacob and Israel; for you are my servant: I have formed you; you are my servant: O Israel, you shall not be forgotten of me. 22 I have blotted out, as a thick cloud, your transgressions, and, as a cloud, your sins:

Return unto me; for I have redeemed you. 23 Sing, O you heavens; for the LORD has done it: shout, ye lower parts of the earth: break forth into singing, you mountains, O forest, and every tree therein: for the LORD has redeemed Jacob, and glorified himself in Israel [in Judah, Jerusalem].

Isaiah 44: 1-23 KJV

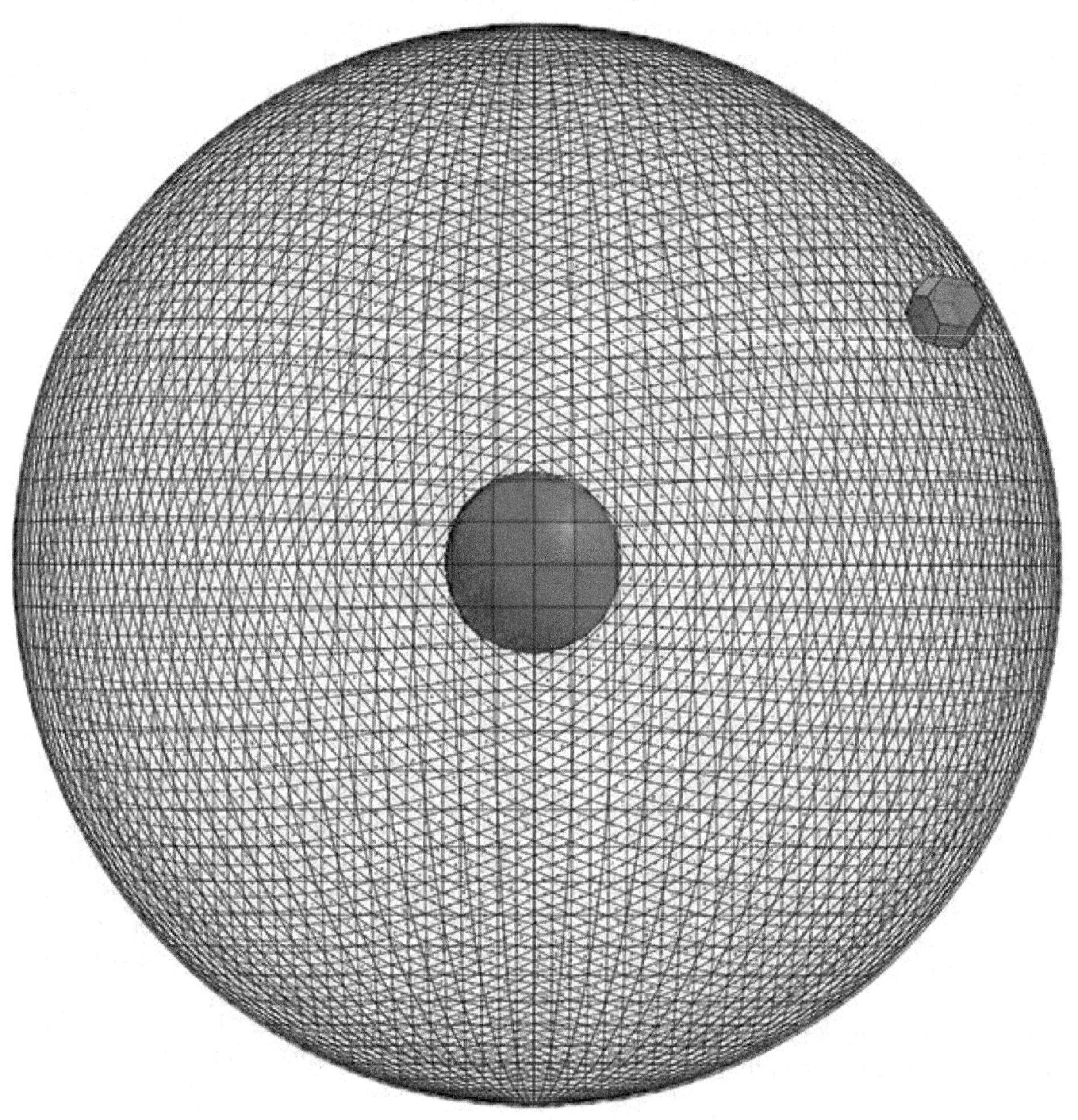

[Hydrogen] Atom Lambda
Sun, bright and morning star.

Revelation 22

Bright and Morning Star

> 24 Thus says the LORD, your redeemer, and he that formed you from the womb, I am the LORD that makes all things; that stretches forth the heavens alone; that spread abroad the earth by myself; 25 That frustrates the tokens of the liars, and makes diviners mad; that turns wise men backward, and makes their knowledge foolish; 26 That confirms the word of his servant, and performs the counsel of his messengers; that saith to Jerusalem, You shalt be inhabited; and to the cities of Judah, Ye shall be built, and I will raise up the decayed places thereof: 27 That saith to the deep, Be dry, and I will dry up thy rivers.
>
> Isaiah 44:24-27 KJV

1 And he showed me [a hydrogen atom], a pure river of water of life, clear as crystal, proceeding out of the throne of God [strong Gravity] and of [Atom Lambda] the Lamb [in the sun].

Blake, Joy on the Morning
Ca. 1803 to 1815

Overhead are angels of light, boson, gluons. The house below represents the brain, wherein is Mary (neutron), Joseph (gluon and baby Jesus, (proton). Below are servants, slaves for the bladder and bowels; mass, light.

2 In the midst of the street of it, and on either side of the river, was there the tree of life, which bare twelve manner of fruits [compilations of energy, mass and light that comprise Judah, Israel, Jerusalem and Ephesus];

And [the tree of life, a hydrogen atom, Atom Lambda] yielded her fruit every** month[1]:

And the leaves of the tree [a balm] were for the healing [the conflict] of the nations [Jewels and the Gentiles].

3 And there shall be no more* curse [that grew out of the sin of Eve and Adam]: but the throne of God and of the Lamb shall be in it; And his servants [that reside in the nucleus of Atom Lambda] shall serve him: 4 And they [his servants] shall see his face [for every face is his face]; and his name shall be in their foreheads.

5 And there shall be no night [ignorance] there; and they need no candle* [photon], neither light of the sun; for the Lord God gives them light: and they shall reign for ever and ever. 6 And he said unto me, These sayings are faithful and true: and the Lord God of the holy prophets sent his angel to shew unto his servants the things

1 In this current age, new fruit is conceived every 12 months or more depending on the cycles of the moon.

Cyrus, the Shepherd

28 That saith of Cyrus, He is my shepherd, and shall perform all my pleasure: even saying to Jerusalem, Thou shalt be built; and to the temple, Thy foundation shall be laid.

Isaiah 44: 28 KJV

"... Whosoever will, let him take the water of life freely ..."

which must shortly be done. 7 Behold, I come
quickly: blessed is he that keeps the sayings of
the prophecy of this book.

8 And I John saw these things, and heard
them. And when I had heard and seen, I fell
down to worship before the feet of the angel
which shewed me these things.

9 Then saith he unto me, See thou do it not:
for I [Jesus Christ] am thy fellow servant, and of
thy brethren the prophets, and of them which
keep the sayings of this book: worship God. 10
And he said unto me, Seal not the sayings of the
prophecy of this book: for the time is at hand.

11 He that is unjust, let him be unjust still:
And he which is filthy [consuming fecal matter
and urine], let him be filthy still: And he that
is righteous [following the Lambda], let him be
righteous still: And he that is holy, let him be
holy still.

12 And, behold, I come quickly; and my
reward is with me, to give every man according
as his work shall be. 13 I am Alpha and Omega,
the beginning and the end, the first and the last.

14 Blessed are they that do his commandments,
that they may have right to the tree of life, and
may enter in through the gates into the city.

15 For without are dogs [photons], and
sorcerers [Z bosons], and [Sardis the Gentiles]
whoremongers, and murderers, and idolaters,
and whosoever loves and makes a lie.

16 I Jesus have sent mine angel to testify unto
you these things in the churches. I am the root
[proton] and the offspring of David [gluon], and
[I am [hydrogen] atom in the sun], the bright
and morning star.

17 And the Spirit [Atom Lambda] and the
bride [Adam, mankind] say, Come. And let him
that hears say, Come. And let him that is athirst
come. And whosoever will, let him take the
water of life freely.

18 For I testify unto every man that hears the
words of the prophecy of this book, If any man
shall add unto these things, God shall add unto
him the plagues that are written in this book:

19 And if any man shall take away from the
words of the book of this prophecy, God shall
take away his part out of the book of life, and
out of the holy city, and from the things which
are written in this book.

20 He which testifies these things saith,

Surely I come quickly. Amen. Even so, come,
Lord Jesus. 21 The grace of our Lord Jesus Christ
be with you all. Amen. ✍

Revelation 22:1-21 KJV

Predestination

Cycle of Births by Force

Mon	Day	Year	Thru	Mon	Day	Year	Forces	Genetic Crop
1	28	1645	–	2	15	1646	strong-Gravity	Judah
2	16	1646	–	2	4	1647	electromagnetism	Gentiles
2	5	1647	–	1	24	1648	electroweak-weak	Jerusalem
1	25	1648	–	2	10	1649	strong nuclear	Israel
2	11	1649	–	2	0	1650	strong-Gravity	Judah
2	1	1650	–	1	20	1651	electromagnetism	Gentiles
1	21	1651	–	2	8	1652	electroweak-weak	Jerusalem
2	9	1652	–	1	28	1653	strong nuclear	Israel
1	29	1653	–	2	16	1654	strong-Gravity	Judah
2	17	1654	–	2	5	1655	electromagnetism	Gentiles
2	6	1655	–	1	25	1656	electroweak-weak	Jerusalem
1	26	1656	–	2	12	1657	strong nuclear	Israel
2	13	1657	–	2	1	1658	strong-Gravity	Judah
2	2	1658	–	1	22	1659	electromagnetism	Gentiles
1	23	1659	–	2	10	1660	electroweak-weak	Jerusalem
2	11	1660	–	1	29	1661	strong nuclear	Israel
1	30	1661	–	2	17	1662	strong-Gravity	Judah
2	18	1662	–	2	7	1663	electromagnetism	Gentiles
2	8	1663	–	1	27	1664	electroweak-weak	Jerusalem
1	28	1664	–	2	14	1665	strong nuclear	Israel
2	15	1665	–	2	3	1666	strong-Gravity	Judah
2	4	1666	–	1	23	1667	electromagnetism	Gentiles
1	24	1667	–	2	11	1668	electroweak-weak	Jerusalem
2	12	1668	–	2	0	1669	strong nuclear	Israel
2	1	1669	–	1	20	1670	strong-Gravity	Judah
1	21	1670	–	2	8	1671	electromagnetism	Gentiles
2	9	1671	–	1	29	1672	electroweak-weak	Jerusalem
1	30	1672	–	2	16	1673	strong nuclear	Israel
2	17	1673	–	2	5	1674	strong-Gravity	Judah
2	6	1674	–	1	25	1675	electromagnetism	Gentiles
1	26	1675	–	2	13	1676	electroweak-weak	Jerusalem
2	14	1676	–	2	1	1677	strong nuclear	Israel
2	2	1677	–	1	22	1678	strong-Gravity	Judah
1	23	1678	–	2	10	1679	electromagnetism	Gentiles
2	11	1679	–	1	30	1680	electroweak-weak	Jerusalem
1	31	1680	–	2	17	1681	strong nuclear	Israel
2	18	1681	–	2	6	1682	strong-Gravity	Judah
2	7	1682	–	1	26	1683	electromagnetism	Gentiles
1	27	1683	–	2	14	1684	electroweak-weak	Jerusalem
2	15	1684	–	2	2	1685	strong nuclear	Israel
2	3	1685	–	1	23	1686	strong-Gravity	Judah
1	24	1686	–	2	11	1687	electromagnetism	Gentiles
2	12	1687	–	2	1	1688	electroweak-weak	Jerusalem
2	2	1688	–	1	20	1689	strong nuclear	Israel
1	21	1689	–	2	8	1690	strong-Gravity	Judah
2	9	1690	–	1	28	1691	electromagnetism	Gentiles
1	29	1691	–	2	16	1692	electroweak-weak	Jerusalem
2	17	1692	–	2	4	1693	strong nuclear	Israel
2	5	1693	–	1	24	1694	strong-Gravity	Judah
1	25	1694	–	2	12	1695	electromagnetism	Gentiles
2	13	1695	–	2	2	1696	electroweak-weak	Jerusalem

Mon	Day	Year	Thru	Mon	Day	Year	Forces	Genetic Crop
2	3	1696	–	1	22	1697	strong nuclear	Israel
1	23	1697	–	2	10	1698	strong-Gravity	Judah
2	11	1698	–	1	30	1699	electromagnetism	Gentiles
1	31	1699	–	2	18	1700	electroweak-weak	Jerusalem
2	19	1700	–	2	7	1701	strong nuclear	Israel
2	8	1701	–	1	27	1702	strong-Gravity	Judah
1	28	1702	–	2	15	1703	electromagnetism	Gentiles
2	16	1703	–	2	4	1704	electroweak-weak	Jerusalem
2	5	1704	–	1	24	1705	strong nuclear	Israel
1	25	1705	–	2	12	1706	strong-Gravity	Judah
2	13	1706	–	2	2	1707	electromagnetism	Gentiles
2	3	1707	–	1	22	1708	electroweak-weak	Jerusalem
1	23	1708	–	2	9	1709	strong nuclear	Israel
2	10	1709	–	1	29	1710	strong-Gravity	Judah
1	30	1710	–	2	16	1711	electromagnetism	Gentiles
2	17	1711	–	2	6	1712	electroweak-weak	Jerusalem
2	7	1712	–	1	25	1713	strong nuclear	Israel
1	26	1713	–	2	13	1714	strong-Gravity	Judah
2	14	1714	–	2	3	1715	electromagnetism	Gentiles
2	4	1715	–	1	23	1716	electroweak-weak	Jerusalem
1	24	1716	–	2	10	1717	strong nuclear	Israel
2	11	1717	–	1	30	1718	strong-Gravity	Judah
1	31	1718	–	2	18	1719	electromagnetism	Gentiles
2	19	1719	–	2	7	1720	electroweak-weak	Jerusalem
2	8	1720	–	1	27	1721	strong nuclear	Israel
1	28	1721	–	2	15	1722	strong-Gravity	Judah
2	16	1722	–	2	4	1723	electromagnetism	Gentiles
2	5	1723	–	1	25	1724	electroweak-weak	Jerusalem
1	26	1724	–	2	12	1725	strong nuclear	Israel
2	13	1725	–	2	1	1726	strong-Gravity	Judah
2	2	1726	–	1	21	1727	electromagnetism	Gentiles
1	22	1727	–	2	9	1728	electroweak-weak	Jerusalem
2	10	1728	–	1	28	1729	strong nuclear	Israel
1	29	1729	–	2	16	1730	strong-Gravity	Judah
2	17	1730	–	2	6	1731	electromagnetism	Gentiles
2	7	1731	–	1	26	1732	electroweak-weak	Jerusalem
1	27	1732	–	2	13	1733	strong nuclear	Israel
2	14	1733	–	2	3	1734	strong-Gravity	Judah
2	4	1734	–	1	23	1735	electromagnetism	Gentiles
1	24	1735	–	2	11	1736	electroweak-weak	Jerusalem
2	12	1736	–	1	30	1737	strong nuclear	Israel
1	31	1737	–	2	18	1738	strong-Gravity	Judah
2	19	1738	–	2	7	1739	electromagnetism	Gentiles
2	8	1739	–	1	28	1740	electroweak-weak	Jerusalem
1	29	1740	–	2	15	1741	strong nuclear	Israel
2	16	1741	–	2	4	1742	strong-Gravity	Judah
2	5	1742	–	1	25	1743	electromagnetism	Gentiles
1	26	1743	–	2	12	1744	electroweak-weak	Jerusalem
2	13	1744	–	2	0	1745	strong nuclear	Israel
2	1	1745	–	1	21	1746	strong-Gravity	Judah
1	22	1746	–	2	8	1747	electromagnetism	Gentiles

Mon	Day	Year	Thru	Mon	Day	Year	Forces	Genetic Crop
2	9	1747	–	1	29	1748	electroweak-weak	Jerusalem
1	30	1748	–	2	16	1749	strong nuclear	Israel
2	17	1749	–	2	6	1750	strong-Gravity	Judah
2	7	1750	–	1	26	1751	electromagnetism	Gentiles
1	27	1751	–	2	14	1752	electroweak-weak	Jerusalem
2	15	1752	–	2	2	1753	strong nuclear	Israel
2	3	1753	–	1	22	1754	strong-Gravity	Judah
1	23	1754	–	2	10	1755	electromagnetism	Gentiles
2	11	1755	–	1	30	1756	electroweak-weak	Jerusalem
1	31	1756	–	2	17	1757	strong nuclear	Israel
2	18	1757	–	2	7	1758	strong-Gravity	Judah
2	8	1758	–	1	28	1759	electromagnetism	Gentiles
1	29	1759	–	2	16	1760	electroweak-weak	Jerusalem
2	17	1760	–	2	4	1761	strong nuclear	Israel
2	5	1761	–	1	24	1762	strong-Gravity	Judah
1	25	1762	–	2	12	1763	electromagnetism	Gentiles
2	13	1763	–	2	1	1764	electroweak-weak	Jerusalem
2	2	1764	–	1	20	1765	strong nuclear	Israel
1	21	1765	–	2	8	1766	strong-Gravity	Judah
2	9	1766	–	1	29	1767	electromagnetism	Gentiles
1	30	1767	–	2	17	1768	electroweak-weak	Jerusalem
2	18	1768	–	2	6	1769	strong nuclear	Israel
2	7	1769	–	1	26	1770	strong-Gravity	Judah
1	27	1770	–	2	14	1771	electromagnetism	Gentiles
2	15	1771	–	2	3	1772	electroweak-weak	Jerusalem
2	4	1772	–	1	22	1773	strong nuclear	Israel
1	23	1773	–	2	10	1774	strong-Gravity	Judah
2	11	1774	–	1	30	1775	electromagnetism	Gentiles
1	31	1775	–	2	18	1776	electroweak-weak	Jerusalem
2	19	1776	–	2	7	1777	strong nuclear	Israel
2	8	1777	–	1	27	1778	strong-Gravity	Judah
1	28	1778	–	2	15	1779	electromagnetism	Gentiles
2	16	1779	–	2	4	1780	electroweak-weak	Jerusalem
2	5	1780	–	1	23	1781	strong nuclear	Israel
1	24	1781	–	2	11	1782	strong-Gravity	Judah
2	12	1782	–	2	1	1783	electromagnetism	Gentiles
2	2	1783	–	1	21	1784	electroweak-weak	Jerusalem
1	22	1784	–	2	8	1785	strong nuclear	Israel
2	9	1785	–	1	29	1786	strong-Gravity	Judah
1	30	1786	–	2	17	1787	electromagnetism	Gentiles
2	18	1787	–	2	6	1788	electroweak-weak	Jerusalem
2	7	1788	–	1	25	1789	strong nuclear	Israel
1	26	1789	–	2	13	1790	strong-Gravity	Judah
2	14	1790	–	2	2	1791	electromagnetism	Gentiles
2	3	1791	–	1	23	1792	electroweak-weak	Jerusalem
1	24	1792	–	2	10	1793	strong nuclear	Israel
2	11	1793	–	1	30	1794	strong-Gravity	Judah
1	31	1794	–	1	20	1795	electromagnetism	Gentiles
1	21	1795	–	2	8	1796	electroweak-weak	Jerusalem
2	9	1796	–	1	27	1797	strong nuclear	Israel
1	28	1797	–	2	15	1798	strong-Gravity	Judah

Mon	Day	Year	Thru	Mon	Day	Year	Forces	Genetic Crop
2	16	1798	–	2	4	1799	electromagnetism	Gentiles
2	5	1799	–	1	24	1800	electroweak-weak	Jerusalem
1	25	1800	–	2	12	1801	strong nuclear	Israel
2	13	1801	–	2	2	1802	strong-Gravity	Judah
2	3	1802	–	1	22	1803	electromagnetism	Gentiles
1	23	1803	–	2	10	1804	electroweak-weak	Jerusalem
2	11	1804	–	1	30	1805	strong nuclear	Israel
1	31	1805	–	2	17	1806	strong-Gravity	Judah
2	18	1806	–	2	6	1807	electromagnetism	Gentiles
2	7	1807	–	1	27	1808	electroweak-weak	Jerusalem
1	28	1808	–	2	13	1809	strong nuclear	Israel
2	14	1809	–	2	3	1810	strong-Gravity	Judah
2	4	1810	–	1	24	1811	electromagnetism	Gentiles
1	25	1811	–	2	12	1812	electroweak-weak	Jerusalem
2	13	1812	–	2	0	1813	strong nuclear	Israel
2	1	1813	–	1	20	1814	strong-Gravity	Judah
1	21	1814	–	2	8	1815	electromagnetism	Gentiles
2	9	1815	–	1	28	1816	electroweak-weak	Jerusalem
1	29	1816	–	2	15	1817	strong nuclear	Israel
2	16	1817	–	2	4	1818	strong-Gravity	Judah
2	5	1818	–	1	25	1819	electromagnetism	Gentiles
1	26	1819	–	2	13	1820	electroweak-weak	Jerusalem
2	14	1820	–	2	2	1821	strong nuclear	Israel
2	3	1821	–	1	22	1822	strong-Gravity	Judah
1	23	1822	–	2	10	1823	electromagnetism	Gentiles
2	11	1823	–	1	30	1824	electroweak-weak	Jerusalem
1	31	1824	–	2	17	1825	strong nuclear	Israel
2	18	1825	–	2	6	1826	strong-Gravity	Judah
2	7	1826	–	1	26	1827	electromagnetism	Gentiles
1	27	1827	–	2	14	1828	electroweak-weak	Jerusalem
2	15	1828	–	2	3	1829	strong nuclear	Israel
2	4	1829	–	1	24	1830	strong-Gravity	Judah
1	25	1830	–	2	12	1831	electromagnetism	Gentiles
2	13	1831	–	2	1	1832	electroweak-weak	Jerusalem
2	2	1832	–	2	19	1833	strong nuclear	Israel
2	20	1833	–	2	8	1834	strong-Gravity	Judah
2	9	1834	–	1	28	1835	electromagnetism	Gentiles
1	29	1835	–	2	16	1836	electroweak-weak	Jerusalem
2	17	1836	–	2	4	1837	strong nuclear	Israel
2	5	1837	–	1	25	1838	strong-Gravity	Judah
1	26	1838	–	2	13	1839	electromagnetism	Gentiles
2	14	1839	–	2	2	1840	electroweak-weak	Jerusalem
2	3	1840	–	1	22	1841	strong nuclear	Israel
1	23	1841	–	2	9	1842	strong-Gravity	Judah
2	10	1842	–	1	29	1843	electromagnetism	Gentiles
1	30	1843	–	2	17	1844	electroweak-weak	Jerusalem
2	18	1844	–	2	6	1845	strong nuclear	Israel
2	7	1845	–	1	26	1846	strong-Gravity	Judah
1	27	1846	–	2	14	1847	electromagnetism	Gentiles
2	15	1847	–	2	4	1848	electroweak-weak	Jerusalem
2	5	1848	–	1	23	1849	strong nuclear	Israel

Mon	Day	Year	Thru	Mon	Day	Year	Forces	Genetic Crop
1	24	1849	–	2	11	1850	strong-Gravity	Judah
2	12	1850	–	2	0	1851	electromagnetism	Gentiles
2	1	1851	–	2	19	1852	electroweak-weak	Jerusalem
2	20	1852	–	2	7	1853	strong nuclear	Israel
2	8	1853	–	1	28	1854	strong-Gravity	Judah
1	29	1854	–	2	16	1855	electromagnetism	Gentiles
2	17	1855	–	2	5	1856	electroweak-weak	Jerusalem
2	6	1856	–	1	25	1857	strong nuclear	Israel
1	26	1857	–	2	13	1858	strong-Gravity	Judah
2	14	1858	–	2	2	1859	electromagnetism	Gentiles
2	3	1859	–	1	22	1860	electroweak-weak	Jerusalem
1	23	1860	–	2	9	1861	strong nuclear	Israel
2	10	1861	–	1	29	1862	strong-Gravity	Judah
1	30	1862	–	2	17	1863	electromagnetism	Gentiles
2	18	1863	–	2	7	1864	electroweak-weak	Jerusalem
2	8	1864	–	1	26	1865	strong nuclear	Israel
1	27	1865	–	2	14	1866	strong-Gravity	Judah
2	15	1866	–	2	4	1867	electromagnetism	Gentiles
2	5	1867	–	1	24	1868	electroweak-weak	Jerusalem
1	25	1868	–	2	10	1869	strong nuclear	Israel
2	11	1869	–	1	30	1870	strong-Gravity	Judah
1	31	1870	–	2	18	1871	electromagnetism	Gentiles
2	19	1871	–	2	8	1872	electroweak-weak	Jerusalem
2	9	1872	–	1	28	1873	strong nuclear	Israel
1	29	1873	–	2	16	1874	strong-Gravity	Judah
2	17	1874	–	2	5	1875	electromagnetism	Gentiles
2	6	1875	–	1	25	1876	electroweak-weak	Jerusalem
1	26	1876	–	2	12	1877	strong nuclear	Israel
2	13	1877	–	2	1	1878	strong-Gravity	Judah
2	2	1878	–	1	21	1879	electromagnetism	Gentiles
1	22	1879	–	2	9	1880	electroweak-weak	Jerusalem
2	10	1880	–	1	29	1881	strong nuclear	Israel
1	30	1881	–	2	17	1882	strong-Gravity	Judah
2	18	1882	–	2	7	1883	electromagnetism	Gentiles
2	8	1883	–	1	27	1884	electroweak-weak	Jerusalem
1	28	1884	–	2	14	1885	strong nuclear	Israel
2	15	1885	–	2	3	1886	strong-Gravity	Judah
2	4	1886	–	1	23	1887	electromagnetism	Gentiles
1	24	1887	–	2	11	1888	electroweak-weak	Jerusalem
2	12	1888	–	1	30	1889	strong nuclear	Israel
1	31	1889	–	1	20	1890	strong-Gravity	Judah
1	21	1890	–	2	8	1891	electromagnetism	Gentiles
2	9	1891	–	1	29	1892	electroweak-weak	Jerusalem
1	30	1892	–	2	16	1893	strong nuclear	Israel
2	17	1893	–	2	5	1894	strong-Gravity	Judah
2	6	1894	–	1	25	1895	electromagnetism	Gentiles
1	26	1895	–	2	12	1896	electroweak-weak	Jerusalem
2	13	1896	–	2	1	1897	strong nuclear	Israel
2	2	1897	–	1	21	1898	strong-Gravity	Judah
1	22	1898	–	2	9	1899	electromagnetism	Gentiles
2	10	1899	–	1	30	1900	electroweak-weak	Jerusalem

Mon	Day	Year	Thru	Mon	Day	Year	Forces	Genetic Crop
1	31	1900	–	2	18	1901	strong nuclear	Israel
2	19	1901	–	2	7	1902	strong-Gravity	Judah
2	8	1902	–	1	28	1903	electromagnetism	Gentiles
1	29	1903	–	2	15	1904	electroweak-weak	Jerusalem
2	16	1904	–	2	3	1905	strong nuclear	Israel
2	4	1905	–	1	24	1906	strong-Gravity	Judah
1	25	1906	–	2	12	1907	electromagnetism	Gentiles
2	13	1907	–	2	1	1908	electroweak-weak	Jerusalem
2	2	1908	–	1	21	1909	strong nuclear	Israel
1	22	1909	–	2	9	1910	strong-Gravity	Judah
2	10	1910	–	1	29	1911	electromagnetism	Gentiles
1	30	1911	–	2	17	1912	electroweak-weak	Jerusalem
2	18	1912	–	2	5	1913	strong nuclear	Israel
2	6	1913	–	1	25	1914	strong-Gravity	Judah
1	26	1914	–	2	13	1915	electromagnetism	Gentiles
2	14	1915	–	2	2	1916	electroweak-weak	Jerusalem
2	3	1916	–	1	22	1917	strong nuclear	Israel
1	23	1917	–	2	10	1918	strong-Gravity	Judah
2	11	1918	–	2	0	1919	electromagnetism	Gentiles
2	1	1919	–	2	19	1920	electroweak-weak	Jerusalem
2	20	1920	–	2	7	1921	strong nuclear	Israel
2	8	1921	–	1	27	1922	strong-Gravity	Judah
1	28	1922	–	2	15	1923	electromagnetism	Gentiles
2	16	1923	–	2	4	1924	electroweak-weak	Jerusalem
2	5	1924	–	1	23	1925	strong nuclear	Israel
1	24	1925	–	2	12	1926	strong-Gravity	Judah
2	13	1926	–	2	1	1927	electromagnetism	Gentiles
2	2	1927	–	1	22	1928	electroweak-weak	Jerusalem
1	23	1928	–	2	9	1929	strong nuclear	Israel
2	10	1929	–	1	29	1930	strong-Gravity	Judah
1	30	1930	–	2	16	1931	electromagnetism	Gentiles
2	17	1931	–	2	5	1932	electroweak-weak	Jerusalem
2	6	1932	–	1	25	1933	strong nuclear	Israel
1	26	1933	–	2	13	1934	strong-Gravity	Judah
2	14	1934	–	2	3	1935	electromagnetism	Gentiles
2	4	1935	–	1	23	1936	electroweak-weak	Jerusalem
1	24	1936	–	2	10	1937	strong nuclear	Israel
2	11	1937	–	1	30	1938	strong-Gravity	Judah
1	31	1938	–	2	18	1939	electromagnetism	Gentiles
2	19	1939	–	2	7	1940	electroweak-weak	Jerusalem
2	8	1940	–	1	26	1941	strong nuclear	Israel
1	27	1941	–	2	14	1942	strong-Gravity	Judah
2	15	1942	–	2	4	1943	electromagnetism	Gentiles
2	5	1943	–	1	24	1944	electroweak-weak	Jerusalem
1	25	1944	–	2	12	1945	strong nuclear	Israel
2	13	1945	–	2	1	1946	strong-Gravity	Judah
2	2	1946	–	1	21	1947	electromagnetism	Gentiles
1	22	1947	–	2	9	1948	electroweak-weak	Jerusalem
2	10	1948	–	1	28	1949	strong nuclear	Israel
1	29	1949	–	2	16	1950	strong-Gravity	Judah
2	17	1950	–	2	5	1951	electromagnetism	Gentiles

Mon	Day	Year	Thru	Mon	Day	Year	Forces	Genetic Crop
2	6	1951	–	1	26	1952	electroweak-weak	Jerusalem
1	27	1952	–	2	13	1953	strong nuclear	Israel
2	14	1953	–	2	2	1954	strong-Gravity	Judah
2	3	1954	–	1	23	1955	electromagnetism	Gentiles
1	24	1955	–	2	11	1956	electroweak-weak	Jerusalem
2	12	1956	–	1	30	1957	strong nuclear	Israel
1	31	1957	–	2	17	1958	strong-Gravity	Judah
2	18	1958	–	2	7	1959	electromagnetism	Gentiles
2	8	1959	–	1	27	1960	electroweak-weak	Jerusalem
1	28	1960	–	2	14	1961	strong nuclear	Israel
2	15	1961	–	2	4	1962	strong-Gravity	Judah
2	5	1962	–	1	24	1963	electromagnetism	Gentiles
1	25	1963	–	2	12	1964	electroweak-weak	Jerusalem
2	13	1964	–	2	1	1965	strong nuclear	Israel
2	2	1965	–	1	20	1966	strong-Gravity	Judah
1	21	1966	–	2	8	1967	electromagnetism	Gentiles
2	9	1967	–	1	29	1968	electroweak-weak	Jerusalem
1	30	1968	–	2	16	1969	strong nuclear	Israel
2	17	1969	–	2	5	1970	strong-Gravity	Judah
2	6	1970	–	1	26	1971	electromagnetism	Gentiles
1	27	1971	–	2	14	1972	electroweak-weak	Jerusalem
2	15	1972	–	2	2	1973	strong nuclear	Israel
2	3	1973	–	1	22	1974	strong-Gravity	Judah
1	23	1974	–	2	10	1975	electromagnetism	Gentiles
2	11	1975	–	1	30	1976	electroweak-weak	Jerusalem
1	31	1976	–	2	17	1977	strong nuclear	Israel
2	18	1977	–	2	6	1978	strong-Gravity	Judah
2	7	1978	–	1	27	1979	electromagnetism	Gentiles
1	28	1979	–	2	15	1980	electroweak-weak	Jerusalem
2	16	1980	–	2	4	1981	strong nuclear	Israel
2	5	1981	–	1	24	1982	strong-Gravity	Judah
1	25	1982	–	2	12	1983	electromagnetism	Gentiles
2	13	1983	–	2	1	1984	electroweak-weak	Jerusalem
2	2	1984	–	2	19	1985	strong nuclear	Israel
2	20	1985	–	2	8	1986	strong-Gravity	Judah
2	9	1986	–	1	28	1987	electromagnetism	Gentiles
1	29	1987	–	2	16	1988	electroweak-weak	Jerusalem
2	17	1988	–	2	5	1989	strong nuclear	Israel
2	6	1989	–	1	26	1990	strong-Gravity	Judah
1	27	1990	–	2	14	1991	electromagnetism	Gentiles
2	15	1991	–	2	3	1992	electroweak-weak	Jerusalem
2	4	1992	–	1	22	1993	strong nuclear	Israel
1	23	1993	–	2	9	1994	strong-Gravity	Judah
2	10	1994	–	1	30	1995	electromagnetism	Gentiles
1	31	1995	–	2	18	1996	electroweak-weak	Jerusalem
2	19	1996	–	2	6	1997	strong nuclear	Israel
2	7	1997	–	1	27	1998	strong-Gravity	Judah
1	28	1998	–	2	15	1999	electromagnetism	Gentiles
2	16	1999	–	2	4	2000	electroweak-weak	Jerusalem
2	5	2000	–	1	23	2001	strong nuclear	Israel
1	24	2001	–	2	11	2002	strong-Gravity	Judah

Mon	Day	Year	Thru	Mon	Day	Year	Forces	Genetic Crop
2	12	2002	–	2	0	2003	electromagnetism	Gentiles
2	1	2003	–	1	21	2004	electroweak-weak	Jerusalem
1	22	2004	–	2	8	2005	strong nuclear	Israel
2	9	2005	–	1	28	2006	strong-Gravity	Judah
1	29	2006	–	2	17	2007	electromagnetism	Gentiles
2	18	2007	–	2	6	2008	electroweak-weak	Jerusalem
2	7	2008	–	1	25	2009	strong nuclear	Israel
1	26	2009	–	2	13	2010	strong-Gravity	Judah
2	14	2010	–	2	2	2011	electromagnetism	Gentiles
2	3	2011	–	1	22	2012	electroweak-weak	Jerusalem
1	23	2012	–	2	9	2013	strong nuclear	Israel
2	10	2013	–	1	30	2014	strong-Gravity	Judah
1	31	2014	–	2	18	2015	electromagnetism	Gentiles
2	19	2015	–	2	7	2016	electroweak-weak	Jerusalem
2	8	2016	–	1	27	2017	strong nuclear	Israel
1	28	2017	–	2	15	2018	strong-Gravity	Judah
2	16	2018	–	2	4	2019	electromagnetism	Gentiles
2	5	2019	–	1	24	2020	electroweak-weak	Jerusalem
1	25	2020	–	2	11	2021	strong nuclear	Israel
2	12	2021	–	2	0	2022	strong-Gravity	Judah
2	1	2022	–	1	21	2023	electromagnetism	Gentiles
1	22	2023	–	2	9	2024	electroweak-weak	Jerusalem
2	10	2024	–	1	28	2025	strong nuclear	Israel
1	29	2025	–	2	16	2026	strong-Gravity	Judah
2	17	2026	–	2	5	2027	electromagnetism	Gentiles
2	6	2027	–	1	25	2028	electroweak-weak	Jerusalem
1	26	2028	–	2	12	2029	strong nuclear	Israel
2	13	2029	–	2	2	2030	strong-Gravity	Judah
2	3	2030	–	1	22	2031	electromagnetism	Gentiles
1	23	2031	–	2	10	2032	electroweak-weak	Jerusalem
2	11	2032	–	1	30	2033	strong nuclear	Israel
1	31	2033	–	2	18	2034	strong-Gravity	Judah
2	19	2034	–	2	7	2035	electromagnetism	Gentiles
2	8	2035	–	1	27	2036	electroweak-weak	Jerusalem
1	28	2036	–	2	14	2037	strong nuclear	Israel
2	15	2037	–	2	3	2038	strong-Gravity	Judah
2	4	2038	–	1	23	2039	electromagnetism	Gentiles
1	24	2039	–	2	11	2040	electroweak-weak	Jerusalem
2	12	2040	–	2	0	2041	strong nuclear	Israel
2	1	2041	–	1	21	2042	strong-Gravity	Judah
1	22	2042	–	2	9	2043	electromagnetism	Gentiles
2	10	2043	–	1	29	2044	electroweak-weak	Jerusalem
1	30	2044	–	2	16	2045	strong nuclear	Israel
2	17	2045	–	2	5	2046	strong-Gravity	Judah
2	6	2046	–	1	25	2047	electromagnetism	Gentiles
1	26	2047	–	2	13	2048	electroweak-weak	Jerusalem
2	14	2048	–	2	1	2049	strong nuclear	Israel
2	2	2049	–	1	22	2050	strong-Gravity	Judah
1	23	2050	–	2	10	2051	electromagnetism	Gentiles
2	11	2051	–	2	0	2052	electroweak-weak	Jerusalem
2	1	2052	–	2	18	2053	strong nuclear	Israel

Mon	Day	Year	Thru	Mon	Day	Year	Forces	Genetic Crop
2	19	2053	–	2	7	2054	strong-Gravity	Judah
2	8	2054	–	1	27	2055	electromagnetism	Gentiles
1	28	2055	–	2	14	2056	electroweak-weak	Jerusalem
2	15	2056	–	2	3	2057	strong nuclear	Israel

Printed in the United States
By Bookmasters